SAN QUENTIN'S FIELD OF DREAMS

INNING	1	2	3	4	5	6	7	8	9	R	H	E
VISITOR												
HOME												

OUTS 0

Strike Three, You're Out!

Baseball at San Quentin: The 2010 Season

Kent Philpott

Earthen Vessel Media

Strike Three, You're Out!
Baseball at San Quentin: The 2010 Season

Copyright © 2021 Kent Philpott

Earthen Vessel Media, LLC
San Rafael, CA

ISBN: 978-1-946794-29-1

Library of Congress Control Number: 2021948353

All rights reserved. Photographs and stories used by permission.
Photographers: Katie L. C. Philpott, Bill Mauck, Scott Ostler

Interior and Cover Design: Katie L. C. Philpott

No Part of this publication may be reproduced, stored in a retrieval system, or transmitted in any form or by any means, electronic or mechanical, including photcopying, recording, or by any information retrieval system, without the written permission of the author or pubisher, except by a reviewer who wishes to quote brief passages in connection with a review written for inclusion in a magazine, newspaper, internet site, or broadcast.

Contents

They Were There	9
How It All Began	18
First Day of Tryouts	22
Second Day of Tryouts	26
Making the Cuts	29
Loss of Youth	32
Pay Back	35
Power and Authority	38
2010 Giants Set	40
The Phenom	42
3% Cut	45
For the Record	48
On a Quest	51
First Inter-Squad Game	54
Drugs in Prison	57
Women at San Quentin	60
Last Practice before Opening Day	63
Opening Day	65
More Opening Day	71
Dishon	75
I Did the Best I Could, Coach!	78
Four Sqeezes	84
Roofs	88
The Experiment	91
A Boycott	95
An Update	97

Bad or Good?	100
Considering Stretch	103
Santa Monica Suns	106
The Field	112
Goodbye Chris	115
Disappointments	118
16 Wins, 10 Losses, 1 Tie	120
Fear Is the Reason	123
Frustration	126
Sports in Prison	129
"I knew the gun was loaded, but I didn't think it'd kill."	132
Having a Mission	135
Guards at the Gates	138
The Last Double Header	141
Oakland	146
Where's Dishon?	150
21 Wins, 12 Losses, 1 Tie	153
A Mother and Daughter	158
Baseball and the Search for Meaning	162

Dedicated to all those who love the game of baseball, inside or outside.

They Were There

What They Say:

The following is from Kevin Driscoll who played on the San Quentin Giants team and is now incarcerated at a California State Prison in San Diego. During his time at San Quentin, he studied law and became a lawyer. He has used his knowledge to help many convicts through the years. We look forward to his release on parole in the coming year or two. Kevin and I have remained in contact over the years as I have with his parents.

Kent,

The 2010 baseball season at San Quentin was a long time ago. My memories, even though not in chronological order, are crystal clear. When we played on the Field of Dreams on the Lower Yard, it was pure baseball. Most of us played a little high school ball, but a decent high school team would probably have clobbered us.

We were inmates with shattered lives: murderers, thieves, and rapists were my teammates. I ended up as Most Valuable Player selected by our only inmate coach, Frankie. It did not start off that way, but this is not a story of my best season where I hit four home runs in about 80 at bats or my pitching that brought us to many victories (we were 23 and 13).

It's more a story of actualization, where we took a simple fundamental game and experienced life while making lasting friendships. I suppose the question is, can life be as easy as a simple game of baseball?

I have not read Kent's book on the 2010 season. I don't need to. I lived it from inside the walls of San Quentin.

Kevin D. Driscoll
August, 2019

When you hear the last of three gates lock behind you, the anticipation ramps up as you are now locked in San Quentin Prison. The long walk around buildings and into the yard at the prison's center is filled with uncertainty. Turning the final corner and walking the 100 or so yards to the baseball field is an experience like no other. Activity everywhere. And lots of noise. Weightlifters, joggers, prisoners milling about. It does not take long to notice the guards in watch towers above the yard, armed and monitoring all

activities. The trash talking begins immediately, as you are this Saturday afternoon's entertainment. Best to get to your dugout, get your baseball cleats on, get on the field, and play catch.

Watching the San Quentin infield/outfield practice, I had the realization that these guys could play. They had a pitcher down in the bullpen throwing hard and poppin' the glove. Our in/out was clean, but any error was met with heckling from guys hanging around the dugout fence and backstop. Had to shut it out and play ball.

I was catching and batting leadoff that day. The walk to the plate to start the game was met with . . . well, let's just say not pleasantries. Before I got into the batter's box I tapped the catcher on the shin guards with my bat and said, "Good luck." I was met with, "Hey man, thanks for coming in." I smiled, gave him another tap on the shin guard, and dug in.

Shane Kennedy
September, 2021

My name is Chris "Stretch" Rich and I was lucky enough to play on the San Quentin Giants baseball team from 2003 through part of the 2010 season. I had many highs and lows while playing for the team, all of which were and are special in my life. Baseball is like that. You have great days and off days. I was always thrust into a leadership role based on my past success in baseball. In a prison environment, any day you can play baseball is a great day. I played for a variety of coaches in the prison, including the founder of the program and many that followed. It was never my place to question the methods of the coaching staff. They were free people coming into the prison, doing the best that they knew how, donating their precious time to allow us to play the game we love. Without them there was no baseball team. None of the coaches were perfect – the players far less so. Let me be clear, the program was never without challenges. That is the greatness of teamwork, that those challenges can be overcome for the greater good of the team. Overall, we were able to pull together and have successful seasons on an ongoing basis.

Though many games were scheduled each season, none of those games were promised to us. Games could be canceled for so many reasons, including but not limited to fog, other weather issues, and inmate count issues. Sometimes it just seemed arbitrary. Personal frustration aside, I always lamented the possible effect it had on the outside teams attempting to come into the prison, fearing that the outside players might get fed up and stop trying to come in to play. It seems none of them ever got thwarted.

The program contributed to my release in 2016. The support that I received from the volunteers coming into the prison in addition to players coming in and expressing a willingness to accept us back into the community always lent hope to the possibility of acceptance and equality. It was always a motivating factor, and it proved to be true. My thanks to all the coaches and players, inside and out, who donated their time to establish the San Quentin baseball program and those who continue to keep it going to this day.

Chris Rich
August, 2019

As one of the coaches of the San Quentin baseball team I was given a rare insight of prison from the inside and the men who populate them. I will be forever grateful to Kent Philpott for giving me the opportunity to be a coach and to have the experiences very few can have. I was a corporate attorney in San Francisco and I played on a baseball team that played in the Q in 1995. Subsequently, I played on many teams and brought several different teams in to play, which I continued to do even after Kent asked me to join the coaching staff in 2009.

Kent has provided a very realistic portrait of prison life through the prism of the baseball program with his day to day account of the 2010 baseball season. His is a tale of the difficulty of creating a successful prison program, not just because of the inherent problems of managing 25-30 men who happened to have shown anti-social behavior in their past and present lives. The problems of keeping the program alive from year to year and dealing with a sometimes hostile set of prison administrators made the job even more difficult.

The treatment of the baseball program by the media normally focuses on the lives of the inmate players, and rightly so. But, Kent's treatment of the subject reflects the difficulty of making the program function from the coach's perspective. There are reasons that there were no other baseball programs in the world like the one in San Quentin and that is because it is so difficult to manage and it is so difficult to recruit competent coaches.

I have managed little league and adult baseball teams for many years and it is never easy. One has to deal with so many difficult personalities and still communicate baseball strategy and teach technique, which is extremely difficult and frustrating. Doing so in a prison is exponentially harder. Additionally, there are two issues that constantly hang over you like the sword of Damocles. First, is the threat of "payback" that Kent discusses. There is the constant fear that that if you do something an inmate doesn't like he can have a friend on the outside retaliate against you or your family. That is a reason cell phones in prison are so dangerous. Also, an inmate can put out a threatening "kite" on the coach guaranteeing he will not be allowed back into the prison again. That is ultimately what happened to Kent and why I took over the program.

Second, is the fear that you will do something that will alienate someone in the prison administration or somehow come into conflict with a guard or an administrator, many of whom are known to be arbitrary and unsympathetic. That is what ultimately did me in several years later. One of those issues that Kent discusses is the question of having one or two teams. It is hard to emphasize how significant that issue is and the conflicts it can cause with the prison administration and the inmates. It was the source of one of my greatest anxieties. Incidentally, I think Kent was correct about whether there should be one or two teams and the prison administration should have deferred to him because of his experience in making the program function. The other great anxiety that Kent discusses and the one that caused me the most problems was the game-day ritual of getting the visiting team cleared through the security gates. Nothing is worse than having to tell a player who has made a great sacrifice to come to the Q that he can't get in because of some screwup.

However, for me incurring these risks and anxieties were worth it because I was able to help bring a few people out of the darkness of prison life and give them some temporary joy and something to look forward to. All prison inmates, men and women, in maximum or minimum security prisons, are basically put in warehouses and forgotten by society. Many people object to giving the inmates any kind of programs to make them better persons and this goes doubly for something like playing baseball. But every inmate is a human being with his own story, personality, and emotions. To help any human being to be able to cope with the drudgeries and darkness of everyday life is a good thing, a wonderful thing.

To expose the public to the humanity of people in prison is also a wonderful thing and Kent Philpott not only spent many years in San Quentin helping to allow inmates to get through the day, but he was helping to expose the humanity of people in prison to the outside public. His book will educate many people outside about the realities and virtues of people inside to the ultimate benefit of both.

Elliot Smith
September, 2021

Excerpt from Bill Mauck's "We Had a Great Time" from his book, *Mr. Bill's Scrapbook*, about 1998, when Kent coached the original team, the Pirates:

It was a cold, cloudy day at San Quentin penitentiary. As my nineteen-year-old son, Michael, and I approached the front gate, I could feel a light drizzle against my face. We were greeted by a guard. He checked our names off the manifest, wanded us down and checked our gear. We walked about 200 yards to the main prison walls, where another guard repeated the same process. We were then directed through a series of electronically controlled steel doors. As the last door slammed behind us, we emerged into a vast courtyard. The mood became dark, almost surreal. To our right were gray buildings, and one had the words "Attitude Adjustment Center" etched on the wall. Instinctively, I knew we did not want to go there. To my right were men in bright orange jumpsuits. I later learned these men were HIV positive.

At the far end of the courtyard was a downhill incline to the whole outdoor recreation area, and at the far side of that was a baseball diamond. As I walked out onto the infield, I could smell the fresh cut grass. I felt my cleats dig into the soft turf. It felt good! It had been a while. My high school friend, Kent Philpott, is a minister in Mill Valley, and he coaches the San Quentin Pirates baseball team.

Kent said the Pirates were scheduled to play the San Francisco Oaks Semi-pro baseball team this day, and the Oaks were going to be short a couple of players. He invited Mike and me to come down for a visit and play in this game.

While Mike and I were warming up with the other players along the right field line, the Oaks coach observed us and made some quick decisions. He determined that Mike would lead off and play second base. I would bat ninth and be dispatched to right field. Right field is unique at San Quentin. There is only about two feet of grass in foul territory along the right field foul line. It them becomes a concrete slab. Right field is short, only about 290 feet to the warning track. Normally, the warning track is dirt. Outfielders can feel their cleats dig into the dirt when they come off the grass, and this lets them know they are about ten feet from the fence. At San Quentin the warning track is asphalt. After the warning track the surface becomes concrete. There is no fence; instead, there are benches and tables. This is special, as it makes it possible for the inmates to sit, enjoy the game, and make helpful suggestions to the opposing team's right fielder.

In right center field is the Indian Nation. They have some tepees, sweat-houses, drums, and fires burning. The Nation is protected by a forty-foot-tall portable handmade screen of woven cloth called the White Monster. The Native Americans' religion says that you can sweat your sins away.

So, here I am, a fifty-eight-year-old man taking my position in right field. Off my right shoulder, I can hear the tom-toms. Thump-thump, thump-thump. My nostrils fill with smoke. My eyes are burning. Off my left shoulder, I can hear the constant chatter of the prisoners. "Hey, Col. Sanders, mon! How 'bout some chicken wings and cerveza for the homeboys in right field." "Hey, mon! Pops don't have no beer; just look at him. He drank it all up already."

I started thinking to myself. Self, you are a first baseman. What the hell are you doing in right field? Then I thought maybe I'll get lucky, and nothing will get hit out here. But baseball has an old and true axiom. It states that the ball will find you. It didn't take long. In the first inning, the Pirates hit three hard ground balls in my direction. I was able to get in front of the ball and hit the cutoff man. Everything was all good until this big left-handed hitter came up and hit a high fly ball to straightaway right field. I raced back. I felt my cleats dig into the asphalt and clank on the concrete. I looked down. The inmates scattered. I weaved my way through the benches, but when I looked back up, I had lost the flight of the ball. The ball landed on a table and caromed off a bench. By the time I retrieved the ball, the runner had rounded third base and was on his way home. Things did not get better. Next, they started hitting balls over onto the concrete in foul territory. Cleats tend to slip and slide on concrete. I didn't catch any of them. I walked and struck out. I began to think that I had swerved into the twilight zone of baseball.

My son, Mike, did much better. He struck the ball hard and made some good plays in the field. When Mike steps into the batter's box, he assumes an open stance, with his feet set about three feet apart. As he stands in, he likes to move his hips from side to side. This drew some interesting comments from some of the more progressive inmates. The San Quentin Pirates had a good team; they beat the Oaks 8 to 2. After the game, the mood was jovial, we shook hands, and exchanged pleasantries. Had this game been played anywhere else, I would not have guessed these men were convicts.

John William (Bill) Mauck
October, 2019

For those of you who love baseball, it will come as no surprise that many of us have a book or two or three or four hidden inside of us waiting to be written. Because that's what it is, it's a love affair, especially with the conditions we played under. But working with Kent Philpot made those conditions bearable. With Kent and the other volunteers, along with the contributions of my brothers inside the walls of San Quentin, our team was able to escape San Quentin and be on a baseball field. That was the mercy that I am on my knees about in memory.

John Neblett
July, 2019

Kent Philpott, the legendary Baptist Street minister who devoted his extra service hours not only developing the raw talented but highly enthusiastic inmates at nearby San Quentin State Prison from his church into semi-pro level baseball players, but also simultaneously taught the general rules and laws of life, good behavior, and the meaning of acceptance of God's presence into one' life, is truly one of the most revered men in the 172 year history of the prison. Although I hold him in the highest respect, darn near akin to love for his personal trust in me, his selfless long hours of work with the incarcerated, and in his ministry devotional to God and duty, I say all this, not as mere hyperbole, fanciful extravagant exaggeration, but because it's all true and verifiable by the inmates decade after decade.

And, not from me, a prison staff member assigned as his superior. Warden after warden, officer after officer, inmate after inmate who came to observe him at work with many unfortunate, sad, often trembling men, were equally amazed how he taught, inspired, and often pleaded the more trouble howto play a major love in his life: baseball, hardball, and, if necessary, with some reluctance, softball.

As a retired professor who joined the Department of Corrections and Rehabilitation in 1998, and remained until 2014 before a second retirement, I often reflect how I defended him, fought for him, always praised and promoted him. Believe me when I say I devote such intense admiration of feelings to only a handful of men and women, and at that, missing maybe one or two fingers. Very few, extraordinarily few, deserve such acclaim. But with jealously rampant, often from minority volunteers who claimed they were more suited than Kent to be the baseball coach because they were of the same color as the inmate, I stood up, pointed, and ordered their asses out of my office. Literally so! In truth, to partly teach that loyalty is almost EVERYTHING, especially in that environment. They knew they never played better than Kent, knew the rules, strategies, and skills more than Coach Philpott, or were able to negotiate more honestly and straightforwardly with the inmates gangs, rivals, and faction than this authentic, genuine, real minister.

In short, no one, absolutely NO ONE, including the warden and his associate wardens dared bad mouth, insult, or question Kent's adherence to San Quentin, or his faithfulness to the inmates in front of me. I would simply respond quietly, "I turned the whole baseball athletic program over to him, because never once in the decade we worked together have I questioned a single decision of his, a single judgment he made. Whatever he asked for, he got. Never once has he lied, disobeyed, disappointed, or embarrassed me. Kent is without reservation or qualification one of the finest men I have ever known, and truly deserves a place in the long history of the prison among its 5 or 6 best.

If he would like me to drive from my home more than a hundred miles away to say all this to just one single person, I'll leave immediately.

Don DeNevi
September, 2021
(Don is 2nd from left , top row, in the picture of the tennis team above.)
(Note: Kent says, No, I did not pay Don for the above!)

1
How It All Began

Tryouts for the San Quentin Giants were set for February 27 and March 6. There had been too much rain to allow us to use the "Field of Dreams," thus we would be on the asphalt, which there is not much of due to the new $165 million dollar hospital the State of California put in for the well being of the convict population.

As far as we know, there is nothing like our baseball program anywhere in the country, maybe the world. Outside teams coming in to play convicts—that is the uniqueness. This is not intramural recreation, convicts playing convicts. Actually, this is the third time in the prison's history that there has been such a thing at San Quentin--once a hundred years ago, then during the 1950s, and now in our era, beginning in 1995, it is happening again.

None of this would have happened without Chaplain Earl Smith, of the Protestant Chapel at the prison. One day in 1995, Chaplain Smith walked into the Catholic Chapel and found an inmate clerk sitting at a desk with a catcher's glove on it. The chaplain asked him if he knew how to use it, and the rest is history. At that point I was already engaged in doing ministry at the prison, and the chaplain knew that I and another volunteer, Dan Jones, were baseball guys and asked us to help with the team in 1997.

Chaplain Smith developed the whole program and guided it for many years, up until his retirement. Again, without Earl Smith, there would not have been a baseball program. So many owe so much to the beloved Chaplain Earl Smith. By the way, Chaplain Smith was also chaplain for the Golden State Warriors, the San Francisco 49ers, and the San Francisco Giants–all at the same time.

All our games are home games; no convict teams come in to play San Quentin. Roughly half our team is made up of lifers, that is, they have life sentences, fifteen to life, twenty-five to live, and there are thirteen men classified as "Close B," which is a custody term meaning they are counted seven times a day, since they have long sentences and are considered possible escapees.

Chaplain Earl Smith and Pastor Kent Philpott

In the San Francisco Bay Area, we are blessed to have the BAMSBL, the Bay Area Men's Senior Baseball League. The league is broken down into age groups, over 18, over 28, over 38, and over 48. There are some ex-major leaguers who play on these teams—the Cubs/Oaks, the Fog, the Mad Dogs, the Mission, Tri-Valley, All Blacks, Nor-Cal Pirates, San Jose Orioles, the Longhorns, Tigers, Sting, Barons, and more. Some are made up of young guys, some old guys.

It is real baseball, too, with umpires, striped fields, and fans.

I am Kent Philpott, age 68[1], pastor for over four decades, now in my 26th year at Miller Avenue Baptist Church in Mill Valley, California. Fifteen years ago, I began managing baseball teams at San Quentin at the request of Chaplain Smith, this after fourteen years doing ministry out of the Garden Chapel at the prison.

Prior to the tryouts, Kevin Laughlin and I met together (Elliot Smith,

---

1 That is, in 2010!

Stan Damas, Len Zemarkowitz, and Mike Deeble could not make it) at Pinky's Pizza in San Rafael to discuss how we would handle the upcoming season. In the past, I have always argued for a larger number of players, while most others thought a smaller number on the team would be easier to manage. My suggestion was that we wait and see how many players came out for the tryouts and go by that. One thing we were sure of—certain players would not be on the team. Some of them we considered to be "poison," and a few others, veteran players, were simply not good enough any longer. Our conclusions were not going to be greeted with smiles, but it would have to be done for the sake of the team as well as for the peace of mind of the coaches

This is the first team Dan Jones and I coached at San Quentin— the 1997 Pirates team, the third year of its existence. Jimbo is at the right of the skull-and-cross-bones flag holding it up. Jason Gottlieb is on his left, and then there is Eugene, #25

2008 San Quentin Giants

West Block, 5 tiers high, is in the background. Philpott is on the right side, front row. Behind him is Stan Damas. On the left, in white Giants shirts are, in front, Len Zemarkowitz, and behind him is Kevin Loughlin. In the white hat, next to Philpott is Country, now at home, a friend I do miss. He was our equipment guy and score keeper for years.

2
First Day of Tryouts

February 27 turned out to be a cold and rainy day, but we went on with the tryouts anyway. About forty men came out. We began by playing catch—pairing the players up. Our coaches walked around with clipboards, noting the ones who could at least throw and catch. What caught my eye was that there were a whole flock of new young guys, mostly black, and some looked like ball players. There were a few guys I cut on that first day—anyone would be able to see that baseball was not their game. There were five of these, older convicts, who wanted to be part of the most elite group in the prison, a team that had received national attention more than a few times.

Making cuts is the most unpleasant part of the process for me, and as head coach it is up to me to do it. It is not enough to post a list of the people who are on the team. Some guys, I had learned over the years, took it way too hard when they could not find their names on the roster.

After an hour of playing catch and rolling ground balls to the guys, we coaches got together and made a list of those we would cut immediately. It was not that complicated, really; a practiced eye can see who might be able to learn and improve in the game—and this is the whole thing. Having baseball skills is fairly clear, and about six guys did not have them.

Gathering the guys up, I called out the names of the six who did not make the cut, and moving away with them a bit, I explained that they did not make the team. A couple complained that they did not get a good look, and I had to tell them that I wished they had the ability to play the game but that it was obvious they did not. First step completed then, the pack was narrowed down some.

Maybe I shouldn't care about the feelings of the convicts and save myself some sleep, but I have not yet gotten that tough. The trick is not to become hard inside, which indeed happens to many of the correctional officers and other staffers at any prison. It has been said that I am hard on the outside but soft on the inside; some say just the opposite. I don't know which it is and really don't care. Maybe if I experienced the anger and rebellion of the convicts as some guards do, I would have to get tough to protect myself. I do not want to romanticize or idealize, something some volunteers do, or develop a "we-they" mentality. Once that happens, the cons too often have their way with the unwary.

Many, if not most, of the men I have known in my years at the prison needed to be right where they were. Some of the world's worst are in prison, and we do not want them out amongst us. Prisons are a wonderful institution; no one would be safe without them. Right, I am no bleeding heart liberal, but I have been accused of coddling the convicts merely by making it possible for them to play the game of baseball. Lots of people want the convicts to be doing hard time, chain gang stuff, to pay for their sins. Sure, I understand, to some degree, the feelings of those who have been impacted by crime. I have been so impacted. But we have hundreds of thousands of men and women in jail, and many of them will eventually get out. Then what? Maybe something happens in prison, something that would never take place anywhere else that might change a heart and mind. I have seen it happen, over and over. Real change, too.

I know for a fact that if I were incarcerated in a prison somewhere for no matter how many years, I would love to be able to play the game I love and will always identify with my childhood. This is a motivator for me, too.

There were times in my life when I could have committed a crime that would have landed me in jail. As a teenager I did some really dumb stuff, some of which did put me in contact with the police. It happens quickly and is irrevocable.

Many, if not most, of the convicts I have known got in trouble when they were drunk, stoned, and stupid—this is a phrase I often use. Sorry to those who might identify with this, but most of us are not too reality-oriented as teenagers. Many of the Giants players over the years had committed a horrible crime at eighteen or nineteen years of age and under the influence—almost always under the influence of something.

It was in 1968 that I first began to go into San Quentin. At first I taught the New Testament in the Protestant Chapel's School of Religion. A new chaplain ended that school and went with a Yokefellow program. At that time most of the convicts were white, tough guys—real sociopathic criminal types. Then in 1972 came the George Jackson shoot out, and all programs ceased for a long while. In 1985, I started volunteering at the prison again and saw that the population of San Quentin had changed completely. Now there were lots of blacks, some Hispanics, very few Asians, and still lots of whites. They were younger, kids who got caught up in being bad because there was not much else to do. To a man, the convicts will tell you it was the drug culture that did it, and it lodged most strongly among those on the margins of society, the so-called underclass, made of mostly of blacks and Hispanics. I am no sociologist or criminologist, but anecdotally I am aware of how things changed.

2009 San Quentin Giants

Mike Deeble is in the white Giants uniform, far right, bottom row is Elliot Smith. Philpott is in the back row, far right blocking out a zero on our scoreboard that was built by "Lefty" under the direction of Chaplain Earl Smith who organized and shepherded the new phase of San Quentin Baseball.

Being a member of the San Quentin Giants was a big deal to the guys out on the asphalt that day. Despite warnings of trying too hard, some of the new guys were throwing all out and it would only be a matter of time before something broke in their arms—happens every year. The real ball players, those who had played the game on the outside, knew better and did not attempt to impress, which impressed us.

After the first tryout, our coaches had a pretty good idea of who would make the team. We boiled the list down to twenty-five cons; the second tryout should determine the final roster.

Coach Stan Damas and Kent surveying the team prospects

3
Second Day of Tryouts

March 6th's weather was better, and we were able to use parts of the field where the rain had not created little lakes. Even more convicts were out now, the word having gotten around. Posters had been placed, thanks to our supervisor Don DeNevi, in North Block and in H Unit. (The total for these two "housing" units, one the traditional cell block and the other a dorm style with double bunk beds, is about 1,800 men.)

The count was now about forty-five, up twenty from the previous week, and some really old guys, not as old as me, but guys way past their prime by a decade or so--well there they were. One guy put his name down as Vito Genavesi and said yes when asked if he were part of that family. We didn't believe it.

The field conditions were so good we did not feel we needed to extend tryouts another week. Our coaches really worked it—throwing, fielding, hitting, base running—pretty good chances to see everyone. We would not want it said that we did not get a good look at everyone.

After nearly three hours of baseball, the coaches retreated to the dugout on the third base side, the Giants dugout, and sat down with our clip boards. The list of guys we thought should make the team was longer than we hoped for in the beginning—twenty-two. Besides that, we knew there would be more convicts showing up for weeks—new arrivals who would manage to talk us into giving them a look.

There were thoughts of shortening the list, but I argued for a larger number. I reminded the other coaches that the previous year, 2009, we had two teams, the Giants and the Pirates, and at the end of the year the Giants had thirteen players and the Pirates eleven. I meant that there has always been an attrition rate in operation, at least that I had observed over the fourteen years that I had been there. This was persuasive, so we carried the lot.

Let me spend a moment more on the attrition rate. Baseball, for one thing, is not an easy game to play. Over the years I have noticed that athletes engaged in and excelled in other sports could not play baseball well. Baseball is a game of unusual skills that must be in combination. Speed, hand-eye coordination, body strength from head to toe, agility, stamina (it is a very long season), and more than anything else, the emotional strength to deal with failure. Baseball, it is often said, is a humbling game. You will be humbled when there you are alone on the field having screwed up. Right in front of your world you drop the ball, strike out with the bases loaded in the last inning, throw the ball away and runners are circling the bases—and for guys who had known little more than continual failure, it could be difficult. Courage may be the single most important element for a baseball player—baseball it is said, is 90% mental, 10% athletic ability. Enough said to see now why there is an attrition rate. And in San Quentin there are other factors at play.

Front of the prison as seen from the East Gate

When a person goes to prison it may be years before he (there is no she at SQ) accepts the fact he is there. It is so hard to come to terms with freedom, family, community, job, love, fun—all being lost. Now a life is shot, the future gone, at minimum marred horribly for all time, and all you have is the ubiquitous ugliness that is prison. Not only is San Quentin ugly and dirty beyond description, but the real awfulness is being with who you have to be with, and there is no way to be alone and apart from the twistedness of life that winds up in our prisons. Therefore, convicts will develop a life of delusion. Guys have told me they can throw a fast ball at 100 miles per hour, or that they played major league baseball, and so on. Delusion, illusion, and confusion—all to find a way to live in ugliness and despair. When the realities of baseball life descend upon the deluded and they are shown up for what they are, they will quit.

Of course, there are the injuries, and we have more than our share, because there is little chance for true conditioning. Then, some will do something dumb and get thrown in the hole—that is, segregation or solitary, for one reason or another. It is not unusual to find that a player has been transferred to another prison, or, and this is the best reason, they were released and are now at home, if they had a home.

The upshot of all this is that we are now carrying twenty-two players.

Below:

Standing on the field with Mt. Tamalpais in the background and the Indian sweat lodge behind the fence on the left

4
Making the Cuts

With the tryouts concluded, everyone was called out to the mound. Important meetings are always held at the mound. The pitcher's mound is almost a sacred place. This is where the pitcher stands and delivers the ball. It is to the mound that the coach walks when he takes the pitcher out of the game or strategy is discussed when a game is on the line. Perhaps the real reason the mound is the place of meeting is because the non-player convicts are then too far away to hear what is going on.

The moment I dreaded had arrived. I knew it meant major disappointment for a number of the veterans, some of whom I had counted as friends. "Friends." It is not so easy to know if someone is really a friend or not. Often what looks like a fairly good relationship dissolves when the "friend" is not getting enough playing time to suit him. In any case, I gathered the group into a tight a circle on the mound so I would not have to raise my voice. I could see a lot of guys in blue silently standing along the fence to hear what was about to happen.

Slowly, firmly, I read the names of the players who had made the team. Nearly every head was down. The level of fear was high. What if they did not make the team? Two of the older guys, both of whom were on the "poison" list, stood away from the group with their arms folded across their chests staring at the ground. They knew what was likely to happen—their names would not be called. Word had gotten around, no doubt, like it always does at the prison, because the prison is a rumor mill. Bad news travels fast.

As much as I wanted some guys off the team, I still felt bad for them. I have a history of flip-flopping, though I hate to admit it. Early on, I learned it is a mistake to change my mind and bring a guy back on the team. Every time I did so, I subsequently paid for it. This time I would not do that.

After the team was announced, I invited those whose names were not read out to come talk with me. As the crowd dispersed, I saw that several who had been cut and had played for me for years were upset. For some time they could not approach me; rather, they spoke with other coaches. After some time, maybe ten minutes, one by one these guys drifted over to me, and one by one I listened to what they had to say.

Three Umpires

Coach Len Zemarkowitz (with the out call) and two inmates, also umpires. Dave, on the right, was the first catcher in this last phase of San Quentin baseball and is now at home.

Behind the fence is the "Indian Nation" and you can just make out the sweat lodge and the fire going to heat up rocks for the lodge. The beating of the tom-toms lends a surreal sense to the experience.

One thought he had a lock on the team because he was a veteran. He felt betrayed, he said, and he knew he was better at his position than any of the new guys. He could not look at me, and there were no tears in his eyes. Another one, a black man, said it was personal. I knew he meant racial. The last two years in a row I had been labeled a racist by some black players who had been kicked off the team for one thing or another. Some of the black players on the football team came to my defense and prevented any trouble from breaking out. The flag football team, the Blues Brothers, is almost all black, and they knew racism was not a tag that fit me.

On the one hand, I felt sorry for the men who did not make the team. The coveted privilege to play baseball while in prison had been lost, and it was a genuine loss, perhaps not like losing a wife to divorce or a parent to death, which happens quite a lot in prison, but a loss nevertheless. They would not be dressed out in San Francisco Giants uniforms on April 17, opening day, when the warden threw out the first pitch, when there was a color guard, and the national anthem was sung. They would not be interviewed by members of the media, or line up along the third base line and be introduced as the 2010 San Quentin Giants Baseball Club. They would not be in the team photo or get individual photo shots I always took and which would also be posted on www.flickr.com for their families to see. These cut players would now be a part of the sad mass of convicts who gathered on the lower yard every evening with little to do.

Below:

Umpires flanking Warden Cullen (middle)

5
Loss of Youth

The names of those who made the team were read aloud, and loudest of all where the names that were not called. It had to be done. I remember the sensation, the flood of emotions that came over me when I knew my reflexes were no longer good enough to get me out of the way of a line drive. In fact, I must think of giving up standing at the 3rd base coaches box; the aging process is forcing me to make the calls from the bench.

One of the easiest ways to deal with loss is the one some of the cut players took—anger—at me. Some of these guys have known me for a decade and a half. For some few maybe, I had become a father figure, a father most of them never had. Doubtless no one would try to harm me, but it was a possibility, and I had already been warned that there could be retaliation if one particular guy did not make the team—and he had not.

One by one, I listened to the complaints and the pleas and did my best to make the reason for the cuts as humanely as I could. I quoted the "great prophet," and yes, I thought some imagined I would mention Isaiah, Jeremiah, or even Mohammed, as there are a couple Muslims on the team. But no, I quoted Clint Eastwood from the first Dirty Harry movie: "A man must know his limitations." It didn't help though; the guys were just going to be mad.

A reservoir of anger, fueled by either booze or dope or combination thereof had led some of the men to prison. Anger management is a course/class most inmates have taken. In fact, if there isn't at least one anger management class listed in a prisoner's file, the parole board is not impressed.

Years ago, I nearly let anger get the better of me right on the field. Two old time convicts, during a practice, were trash talking each other. One was near the mound; the other was sitting in the dugout. I had been hitting ground balls to the infield and moved in between the players to see if I could get them to quiet down. One priority I always carry with me is, keep the program alive.

**Johnnie, Giants catcher, hard-core player,
gives it his all every day.**

One incident and Sacramento could close it all down. The argument continued and got louder and louder. The guy in the dugout then shifted focus and started in on me. It was like a trigger was pulled and I started advancing on the player with the bat in my hand. Yes, I will sometimes forget where I am. Just as I was crossing the third base line, another player rushed up and grabbed me, bear hugged me, and stopped me. All of a sudden, I woke up and realized what a huge mistake was in the making. None of this had gone unseen. Probably as many as four officers were watching, one right above us in a gun tower. This same player I was going after is still at San Quentin, and we laugh about the incident once in a while.

Eight guys who were counting on making the team did not. In a certain sense it signaled the end of their youth, even for those who were fifty plus years old. As long as you can play baseball you are not old—this may be what some think, and in prison a convict is frozen solid with the fear that his life is slipping away little by little. It is the worst nightmare.

Below:

Giants and visiting team gathered for pre-game discussion and instructions.

6
Pay Back

March 6 was a Saturday, and Monday morning early I got a call from the prison. My boss wanted me to come in for a meeting. There had been some complaints made about me over the cutting of veteran players. This would not be the first time on this exact issue—I had been expecting such a move. In fact, a group of the cut veterans demanded there be a second team like there had been in 2009. (Ironically, the two teams season was of my own creation.) I had been given a heads up on the demand by Don, my immediate supervisor, a state employee and the person who had developed the prison's recreation program into the success it is today.

To that meeting I brought with me a copy of a paper I had prepared—a one page statement that clarified my action. After reading the paper, the people who supervise the recreation program supported me.

The last thing I wanted was a second team. The trash talk, the ugly, mean attitudes—I had been through it before, and I would not, could not, deal with it again. As best I could I challenged or denied each and every point I knew was going to be brought up. At the same time, I gave into some. There could be a second team but supervised by one of my coaches, the team would not play outside teams, would not be the Pirates and wear the old uniforms, but they could have every other Monday evening and every Saturday evening to practice and play intra-mural games. There was also one big No! on my part---this second team would never play the Giants.

The bottom line with me was to keep the program up and running. It would not take much to close it down. One fight on the field, or in North Block, or in H Unit, and that would be it. Besides, I had already been informed that one of the veterans who was cut—a pitcher—had already boasted he was going to be throwing bean balls at the Giant players when they played us. (This same player, sadly delusional, demanded that once cut his old uniform must be retired. He had played for a few years but was a marginal player. Such is the depth of the mind-bending that goes on with some convicts.)

It had been said that I was a bit belligerent with the cut players. Perhaps I had been, but now two weeks later, things have already smoothed out some. Let me defend myself: I cannot take any garbage from the players. Because I don't, it has allowed me to be at the prison for twenty-eight plus years.

Don with the tennis racket, is my immediate supervisor, a state employee. He is responsible for developing the unique recreation program at the prison. I am the cool dude in the shades, Stan is to my right. Far left is Chris Rich, who as a college student was a nationally recognized pitcher. The three black men in the center played for the Blues Brothers 8-man flag football team I organized six years ago.

If I give in, I will be taken advantage of and most importantly, lose the respect of the convicts. The same goes for any convict. If one is found to be weak, he will be taken advantage of, and it could be of a sexual nature. Sex is always just under the surface. Every once in a while, we hear of someone being taken out of the prison in hand cuffs—correctional officers, volunteers, state employees—and the reason could be from a long list, but mostly it has to do with drugs being brought in, cell phones, cigarettes, sexual contact, and so on.

What I am afraid of is having drugs, a weapon, or other contraband placed in my equipment bag and then discovered by a guard at a gate. It has happened before and could be so easily done. The result would be a ban on me ever coming into the prison again—no jail time or even an arrest, likely, but embarrassment and shame for sure.

At yearly volunteer meetings the stern warning is given to be wary of getting a phone call with the caller claiming that our families will be safe and we can make extra money, *if* we simply bring something like a thermos into the prison once a month and leave it unattended somewhere for a while and then take it home again. We have a choice then. Do it and eventually be found out and end up in a prison cell. If we do not, we will be going on the witness protection program and be forced to move somewhere.

Pay back can happen.

Right: Kent and Kevin conferring

7

Power and Authority

The meeting about the second team went well, and all sides agreed to the deal. There would not be another team, yet there would be a group of players, those who did not make the team along with some others who might not have been confident enough to try out for the Giants, who would play intramural baseball.

There was no choice, simply because I was not going to go along with the agenda the rebel convicts wanted. One of the troubles with being a coach is you have a certain amount of power, and that power can be easily abused. Over a fifty-year span, I have coached many baseball teams, of many different descriptions, and I have abused my authority on occasion. Additionally, I have seen other coaches abuse players verbally and physically. This is nothing new, but I hate to find it in myself. I am pastor of a Baptist Church with some forty-two years of ministry behind me, and I am fully aware of how quickly spiritual authority can be abused—and I have done it. Now I was in a situation where my demands almost seemed to me to be abusive. I wondered if I was exerting my authority unjustly. In the meeting I brought this issue up to see what others thought. After some very candid discussion, a conclusion was reached that there was really no other way around it. There would not be two teams; there would be the Giants and intramural baseball. Still I am not completely convinced I did the right thing.

Studies have shown it is the human tendency to abuse others under our authority. Circumstances will arise where decisions have to be made and authority must be exercised. And the best of us can fall right into the trap.

How many grew up being abused? It is no doubt safe to say that being abused, bullied, and treated badly by people in authority over us, like parents, teachers, coaches, cops, and so on, will impact and to a significant degree. How many convicts were abused as kids? It creates all kinds of negativity like not caring, being angry and vengeful, and needing to escape a horrible reality with a little help from pharmaceuticals. If I abuse the authority I have, what separates me from the problem?

If the prison system, all parts of it, were to operate smoothly and justly—well, it simply cannot, so don't bother asking the question. Every system devised by humans will be faulty, and very often corrupt and brutal. However many watchdog structures may be in place, abuse of authority will continue, and it does big time at San Quentin. Sorry, warden.

The season is coming up, so the side issues—the rebel cut veterans—must not side track from the work that looms. Practice and more practice, scrimmages, work on defense, bunting, pick-offs, and so much more. Baseball is filled with thousands of details, nuances that usually go over the head of the average fan, but they are there, and I burn to teach them. It will not be as I hope, since there is not enough time, too many distractions and bureaucratic blockages, but on April 17 we play Elliot Smith's Cubs/Oaks and we must be ready.

2009 Team photo of the Pirates

That year we had two teams, the Giants and the Pirates. The Pirates was the original name of the team in the most recent renaissance of the baseball program. At the far left are Len (in black), Stan (in white), then far right is Philpott. The fellow to my right, new player, not sure what he is doing. Hoping it was not some kind of gang sign. This was the very team that beat the mighty Giants at the end of the year. Dave Baker is the big white guy in the middle, back row, team captain and team chaplain. Two players to my right is Henry, the guy whose hit, maybe home run maybe double, won the big game. Len is managing the rebel team. And we all thank him very much.

8
2010 Giants Set

The team was set, but not set. In the course of one week, seven new inmates wanted to try out. For many years my procedure has been the same—play catch with the prospect. I say, "Take this glove, I've got mine, let's go out to left field and play catch. And you will have to be a phenom to make the team." Now, a phenom, as in phenomenal, is a person who is so good we absolutely must have him on the team. To be a phenom you must either be one heck of a pitcher or short stop or center fielder or catcher.

Up the middle—these are the positions that demand the highest priority. And a phenom must be able to hit, since these position players are usually the best athletes. But—this is not always true.

Now I have a man, a convict, and he is scared, anxious, tense, and he wants to impress me. First off, I tell him to throw easy. I tell him I will know if he can play simply by watching the way he throws not how hard he throws. Despite my instruction, many a man, as I have already stated, has done his arm some damage hoping to dazzle the coach with a fast ball or sweeping curve. A rotator cuff is torn, a bicep muscle even torn, and that is the end of it. Sadly, the would-be player turns away in discouragement. It is form, balance, and proper technique that matters to a coach. Some pass the playing catch test, and then I lead them to the dugout and grab a bat. "Show me your swing. Show me how you bunt."

Usually, for a convict who has been down for a long time, I am going to see a softball swing, an upper cut, for the right hander, where the right wrist shifts low with the left wrist on top for a smooth lift swing. Great for a softball player, disaster for a baseball player. I am hoping to see a short, compact and level swing through the zone with the head in. One guy had it, too, a white guy, big tough looking tattooed gang banger. Then he told me he could pitch so we went back to the bull pen, and he in fact had good balance and an easy motion. His stretch was solid; he kept the ball low; he was a phenom. Later on in the practice he hit a ton and played a smooth first base. Now a confession: he had no cleats, only prison issue slippers. The very next practice I brought him in a size 13 shoe, from the San Francisco Giants. Don't tell anyone.

Twenty-two players made the team. Too many, for sure, and I was taking a bit of guff from some of the players as well as from a couple of coaches. I understood—it is not easy to juggle so many players who all would want more playing time. Yet I knew something from my long experience at the prison—there would be a significant attrition rate. There would be injuries, there would be transfers to other prisons, but most of all, players would quit once they saw they would not be starters. At the same time that I announced who would be a Giant, I also said that by June 15 I expected there would be only sixteen players left on the team.

Inside of two weeks, the team was reduced to eighteen players. One went to the hole, solitary, for trying to sell pictures hanging on the chapel wall to volunteers. He is gone, but not before I bought him a pair of $60 cleats, since he wore a size 7.5 shoe and none of the San Francisco Giants have such small feet. Then another one was caught stealing other convict's personal property out of their lockers in H Unit. Another twisted his ankle badly playing basketball, and then one fellow, who could probably see he would not get much playing time, simply stopped showing up at practices. From twenty-two to eighteen. Can sixteen be far behind?

9

The Phenom

A potential phenom showed up. Black guy, skinny, older, but as I took him through the usual paces, I could quickly see he was, or had been, a ball player. And he played short. A potential phenom? Maybe. Like the pitcher in the previous chapter, he had no cleats but played short almost flawlessly in state brown boots. Now, don't let on, but I have a pair of cleats in my equipment bag for him right now.

Lamarr was either the real deal or a good actor. Mister friendly and cooperative, he was never idle. He had plenty of questions about the technique of playing his position or hitting, lots of smiling, hustling, with encouraging comments to others.

He would be competing with a player who had earned the nickname, "Cry Baby." The convicts called him that behind his back, because with the guy's wild side you never knew. I knew he was a whiner and had debated with myself and the other coaches whether he should be on the team despite the fact he is undoubtedly one of the most skilled players and the starting short stop for the last two years. He also pitches. He hits home runs. I was really hoping the new guy would be an unquestioned phenom.

With a pair of expensive but slightly used cleats, the new man, Lamarr King, played fairly well at short during a scrimmage game. Though he had a softball swing, he managed to hit a line drive over the head of the center fielder and make it all the way to third base. Not bad at all. He was smooth and confident making the double play—not a super strong arm but adequate. Cry Baby was noticeably concerned.

For an inter-squad scrimmage game—the potential phenom was not on the starting team but on the second. Before the game, I made it clear that the two team's makeup was only an experiment and things could easily change. Everyone's job was on the line. It was at once a challenge and also a hope, a challenge for the mostly veteran starters, as they could not rely on mediocre play, and a hope for the non-starters that they could move up.

While Cry Baby was pitching, the right fielder dropped an easy fly ball, which produced complaining and blaming, pitcher to fielder. Then, an inning later, the whining pitcher threw a comebacker into centerfield instead of to the second baseman who was covering to start a double play. Again, blaming and gesturing, to the point one of the coaches had to walk out and settle things down.

Now I must make some kind of decision about who plays short, the phenom or the cry baby veteran. (Both are the same race, which makes it easier.) It is only a matter of time though before there will be an explosion on the field during a game against an outside team. It would mean a suspension for the player at minimum and maybe an end to the whole baseball program. Of course, the treasured team chemistry the coaches have been trying to build will be damaged. One person who is allowed to get away with poor behavior can alter the peace of a team. As I write this, I am unsure what to do.

Lamarr King

To complicate matters, one claims to be a Christian, the other does not. Guess which is which? Do I favor my whiner brother? Of course, all I have to go on is the one's statement and the other's silence. This particular dilemma has come up before. Over the year, Christians on the teams have not made an issue over shared faith. In fact, most have been quite good and quiet about it. I am not so sure this time.

Stan Damas and Lamarr

This is being written on a Wednesday, a practice day, and on Saturday there will be another pre-season scrimmage. I think I will set an entirely different, somewhat mixed, starting team and leave our whiner off it. Then I will see what happens. I am hoping the veteran will step up and support my decision. The phenom, though, has not proven, at least so far, to be a real phenom. He has, however, managed to win the respect of most others on the team. He comes to practice early, works on the field, works hard, and quietly goes about his business. Truth is, the team will need both players over the course of the season.

A note about Stan Damas: Stan was my good friend, a retired San Francisco cop, much loved by the guys at SQ. He died some years back, and I will forever miss him.

Below:

Running to get the ball in center field with the Indian sweat lodge seen behind the fence

10
3% Cut

One of my jobs is to set the schedule. This year there was a possibility we would play as many as sixty games. Within two weeks, after I sent out a blanket email to all the managers of the outside teams, the game dates were taken. Thank God for the internet and email. The way it was broken down was the Giants would play Wednesday and Thursday nights and Saturday mornings. Then it was announced, via an email that had originated from the warden's office, that due to a mandatory cut in the California State budget, all program costs had to be reduced by 3%. A whole slew of teachers working at the prison were let go, and how it impacted me was that the Wednesday games were taken away because of imposed staffing shortages—there would be no lower yard officers available on Wednesdays. Thank God again for email—within a couple of days I had the schedule reconfigured. But this morning I received word, via email of course, that there was a change. Thursday would be taken and Wednesday given back. No explanation was given. No sorry was spoken. Oh well.

It is not a big deal, but I am having ("having" meaning not done yet) to do the schedule all over again. The managers of the outside teams might think I am losing it. Maybe they would be right.

The new schedule will be games every other Monday night (the rebel team has the other Monday evenings), Wednesday night, and Saturday morning. My favorite games are on Saturday morning when we will usually play a nine-inning game. Soccer commences at 1 p.m., so if we get going around 10 a.m., we can usually get in a full game. On the weekdays, however, the best we can do is six, maybe seven innings.

My anxiety level goes up every game day. Losing is not the issue, not for the players either. My worry has to do with whether the visiting outside team will be cleared in or not. One time, and this was the worst, a team came up from Los Angeles, came up the day before the game, a Friday, stayed overnight, showed up at the East Gate promptly at 8:30 a.m. Saturday morning, only to find that there had been a racially motivated fight on the lower yard and that the prison was completely locked down—nothing would happen. I went through the motions of talking to the watch commander, mostly to show the visiting team that I tried. It was to no avail, and the disappointment they felt was unleashed on me in the parking lot. They did not realize the chanciness in coming to a prison expecting a baseball game.

Another time a team came up from San Jose. The manager called me a day ahead to make sure the game was on. I called the people who handle such things and was told the San Jose team had been cleared in. But when they showed up on the appointed Saturday morning, the officer at the East Gate could not find their names in his computer. (The next day it was discovered that instead of each player being entered into the computer by name, the entry was under the team name—an unusual and unexpected way to do things.) No game, and this time the players were really mad. Words were exchanged, and I had to repent later on. So, before every game my anxiety level gets turned up a notch or two.

Once in awhile I will ask myself—what are you doing, Philpott? My answer is multi-faceted. One, I was asked to coach baseball by the chaplain many years ago. I said yes, and I want to stick by my word, not that I stick by all my words, but I make the effort. Two, I love baseball, and this allows me to stay around the game. Three, after years of volunteering at the prison, I found that being with the men on the yard directly over the course of many months resulted in getting to know individuals in a way that had been impossible before.

The State of California, particularly the California Department of Corrections and Rehabilitation, was forced to reduce their budget by 3%. If the number had been 5%, that would have been the end of the baseball program. If the state's financial condition does not improve by June 30, then the 3% cut could go to 5%.[1]

---

1   The state's financial situation did not improve, but somehow no further programs were cut.

Left: Kevin Loughlin, great coach and friend, a real baseball guy, and much loved by the team.

Below: Coach Kevin talking with the team before the game starts.

11
For the Record

Before I retire the subject of the 3% cuts, a few more comments—for the record.

The prison has no way to get our uniforms washed. Seems, for cost cutting, the laundry is sent to Solano Prison. My guys tell me it is a disaster, and most of them have gone to washing their own clothes—in their cells. As noted previously, convicts have been known to steal, and it has sadly been discovered that some mesh laundry bags sent out to Solano have been tampered with—and baseball uniforms might seem likely targets.

Then there are no lawn mowers to cut the Field of Dream's grass. Yes, Field of Dreams. About 2001, the wonderful San Francisco Giants, and we are all die-hard Giants fans and know all the stats, gave us their lawn when they put new turf in, and even sent in their experts to do it for us. (We do thank our beloved chaplain Earl Smith, now retired.)

There is no way to cut the grass, though. At the conclusion of the last meeting to discuss the expectations of the rebel team, I was informed that we needed two lawn mowers to cut the grass. I raised my hand. One day later, my wife Katie, whom many of the convicts knew due to her preaching and singing at the chapel and most recently sitting beside me keeping score during an actual ball game—she, when I told her about the need, refurbished an extra gas-powered mower we had. And it works—one pull. This will be her ticket into the opening day seat right next to me in the San Quentin Giants dugout—if the warden approves.

The above might make it seem that I am critical of the way California administrates prisons. This is not the case. Being around convicts is not simple or pleasant. There is not the slightest thing romantic, interesting, or exciting about it—after some period of time. Over the years, I have seen young seminary students take jobs at the prison, and it has ruined more than one of them, at minimum diverted them from their original goal of pastoral ministry.

Those most closely connected with the convicts are the guards, or more properly, the correctional officers. Some are mean and angry people; I understand how they might have gotten that way. San Quentin is a miserable place, and the convicts are most often transformed, if indeed any transformation occurs, into miserable people. Who wouldn't fall prey to adopting what has been called The San Quentin Way? It can be said that to stay in one piece means you have to become hard and mean, self-protective to the point of being brutal. It then follows that the worst thing about the prison is the people who are there, people you cannot avoid but have to live with every day—the crazy people, the sick people, the hardcore criminals, people who will do about anything to satisfy themselves.

Correctional officers deserve and receive my respect, even the ones who think people like me and my baseball program should be barred from the prison completely. Then there are the administrators, the warden's office. A few years ago, there were four different wardens in a six-month period. What a job! On the one hand you have 6,000 convicts to deal with. It is a logistical nightmare; I know this for a fact, but I will not go into it. There are the budgetary concerns, policy issues, the need to protect the public from the convicts, which are called "custody" matters, and then there are all the convict rights that have been evolving over the years. Convicts can "write up" the guards and other prison officials. I can be written up by a disgruntled convict, and I am shocked I have not been already. Every weekday morning the prison's visitors parking lot is flooded with lawyers, visitors, and advocates of various sorts, who put pressure on the warden's office to accommodate them or else face complaints that would likely be taken seriously in Sacramento. The whole thing is a mine field.

What I do with the convicts and playing baseball is a privilege and not a right. My experience has been that the prison has bent over backwards to see the sports programs go on. The kindness of some of the state employees and the guards has been exceptional. I am not being political here, either. I don't have to play that game. But I do see what goes on, and I refuse to adopt the usual view the convicts have about prisons and cops and judges and so on. I have seen volunteers take up the convicts' cause and espouse the typical we/they mentality, which has led to dangerous behavior.

**View of the field looking west,
with Mt. Tamalpais in the background**

View of the prison from the staff parking lot

12
On a Quest

Convicts, especially lifers and three-strikers,[1] will seek out a mission, a dream, a goal, so they can keep alive and sane. Lifers, maybe seven years to life, fifteen to life, twenty-five to life, and simply life, along with three-strikers, who can have sentences of more than fifty years, ordinarily do not adjust quickly to institutional life.

Convicts with death sentences have perhaps the worst time of it. It is not an easy thing to accept that you are never going to live as a free person again, that you are going to live the rest of your life inside a cage, even live with the possibility the state may put you to death.

A mission may be no more than killing the guard, or the guy in the next cell, or finding a way to kill oneself. Thousands of missions have been generated in the minds of those who must find some way to deal with the darkness that has descended upon them, even when that darkness is of their own doing. A mission, at best, is a quest to do something, whether that be good or not.

When a condemned man comes into the prison at San Quentin, he is placed in the Adjustment Center, a prison within a prison, the place where the worst of the worst go. A convict may be there for years, because it takes years to get his attitude adjusted to the fact he will never be free again and that he may well be executed. On a few occasions, I have seen a man being escorted in chains into the Adjustment Center. I have also seen them secured to wheelchairs and carefully taken through the center's small door. A major part of the adjustment must be developing a mission, a reason to stay alive.

---

1   California's Three Strikes sentencing law was originally enacted in 1994. The essence of the Three Strikes law was to require a defendant convicted of any new felony, having suffered one prior conviction of a serious felony to be sentenced to state prison for twice the term otherwise provided for the crime. If the defendant was convicted of any felony with two or more prior strikes, the law mandated a state prison term of at least 25 years to life.

During the years that I visited the blocks with the Man-to-Man prison ministries, I would sometimes hear newly incarcerated men yell out, "I don't belong here!" or "This was not supposed to happen!" On a few occasions, I followed the screams to the very cell and attempted to talk to the frightened man. From the depths of human emotions streamed out a torrent of regret, fear, and confusion—high states of anxiety, with some actually teetering on the brink of a psychotic break. Often the most desperate, the most distraught, were men who looked somewhat like me. No tattoos, no piercings, and without the prison facial hair and hair cuts that one sees on most convicts. I would look into the eyes of someone like myself, and I knew it was likely someone with four-plus DUIs or a domestic violence "beef." Without a mission, a man might go crazy.

Many of the convicts are medicated to help them make the necessary adjustments. Receiving "meds" might be at their own request; sometimes required. Often, just after count clears,[2] I will see the medical people coming out of North Block having completed their rounds of dispensing medications. I have been in North Block while the count was being made and have witnessed the distribution of medications. The free persons, some men, some women, make sure the medication is swallowed.

Being on the baseball team may be the mission for some. Being a Giant is an identity mightily sought for and coveted. To be rejected from being on the baseball team may actually be experienced as an attack upon their coping mechanism. I have noticed that it is almost always the lifer who makes the team his mission. Guys with short sentences do not take the game as seriously as the others.

It is not lost on me as men either make or are cut from the baseball team that missions are at stake. I am conscious of the impact the whole process may have on a man. Am I a counselor, a minister, a pastor, a chaplain, or am I the manager of a baseball team? After all these years I have yet to figure it out.

---

2   Convicts throughout the state are counted a number of times during the day. At 4 p.m. every day throughout the state, each convict must be counted in person, face to face. This process takes roughly a half hour, and after the "count clears" the ball players can be released early from their cells and proceed down to the lower yard for practice or a game. Those that are classified Close B have a higher custody status than others and may be counted seven times a day. Close B convicts usually have lengthy sentences and thus are considered at greater risk for attempting an escape.

On a Quest   53

Players in the dugout on the 3rd base side

13
First Inter-Squad Game

On March 27, a Saturday morning, we had our first inter-squad game. There were enough players to make it happen, but just barely. Selecting the teams was, in effect, a statement as to the makeup of the team in terms of who would be considered starters at that early point.

Earlier I talked about the first scrimmage game, but here I want to revisit it in order to tell a slightly different story—one that will reveal the mindset of some of the convicts.

Playing on an actual baseball team is much different from playing other prison sports—the intramural teams for example, which are common in many prisons across the country. The San Quentin Giants is a real baseball team, and our coaches treat it as such. We ignore, as best we can, the reality that the players are convicts and that our diamond is inside an actual prison. We are not cops, counselors, or chaplains—no, we are baseball coaches. It all goes toward making the SQ Giants baseball real baseball.

When I read out the teams, I made it clear that the team Kevin would manage we considered starters at that point. The team I would take consisted of the back-up players. I explained that nothing was set in concrete, and those players on Kevin's squad should not consider that they had a lock on their status, nor should the players on my team consider that they would not get a lot of innings or not be able to move up.

We played our game, due in part to some of my small-ball managing, like a suicide squeeze with two outs and two strikes on the hitter, and the back-ups won the game.

The reaction to the win on the part of my group amazed me. It was an overreaction and looked like we had won a major competition. Way too much cheering and high fiving.

At the next practice, after all the players had finally gotten to the field, coming in little bunches over the course of an hour, not due to anything on their part but due to it just being the way things go, I noticed that two players did not show up.

Two more players gone, and both were from the back-up group. They had decided to play softball, because, as it was reported to me, "They were only on the 'B' team." Other players had attempted to talk them out of it but to no avail. One of the players struggled to play the game at all and had been receiving extra coaching by coaches and players alike. The second absent player was sure to get a lot of playing time, but he played behind a man twenty years his junior who was acknowledged to be one of the best players on the team. So much for my little speech at the beginning of the scrimmage.

My reaction to the loss of two more players was that we were rapidly moving toward my prediction that by June 15 we would have sixteen players on the team.

I hate to lose ball players for any reason. As I write this, I am feeling the loss. And not to be neglected, I am bound and determined to get the cleats and gloves back from the players. They will probably be sold, however, "off the tier."

Mike Deeble, one of our outside coaches, playing on the Giants team, hits a line drive. Len Zemarkowitz is umping, Johnny Taylor catching, and the guy with the white hat on observing is Scott Ostler of the San Francisco Chronicle, covering the game.

Left and below:

Frankie Smith, one of our inmate coaches

14
Drugs in Prison

How do drugs get into prisons? Lots of ways, starts the answer. Visitors bring drugs in, and I am not going any deeper into this, because if I did, some readers might be offended. State employees, volunteers, and correctional officers bring in drugs, too. The flow of drugs is unstoppable. I have known some convicts who injected heroin regularly, almost openly. It is not uncommon to catch a whiff of grass in the air. One player showed up at a game drunk—pruno was the cause of his intoxication. Pruno is a wine-like beverage that the convicts make themselves, and it is made by the gallons, all the time. One favorite hobby of some is trading pruno recipes.

Smoking is prohibited on state property, and the prison is state property. Even guards have to walk outside the prison to smoke by the East Gate, the real front door to San Quentin. Because cigarettes are no longer sold at the canteen, they have become a major means of currency. The prices of many things are measured out in numbers of packs of cigarettes.

Food items are also used as currency—candy is big, anything sweet, or peanuts. Favors will be paid off with food and cigarettes.

Dope smoking—imagine the value of an ounce of marijuana—so easy to conceal and bring in and pass on. Heroin, cocaine, downers and uppers—all easy to get in, and the amount of tax free money earned by the mules can be large.

Here is one way contraband finds its way into the prison: Someone who regularly comes into the prison (called a "mule" in our example) can be contacted by a person who is willing to pay a substantial amount of money for whatever can be brought in. For instance, for bringing in an ounce of marijuana, $500 might be made. The mule would receive the money in the mail, or it could be dropped off at the house. There are many schemes working all the time.

Convicts often have real cash, too, hidden away on their person. Cash comes in like drugs and cigarettes and other contraband items.

Cell phones are prized. During the season a sweep was made of North Block. The residents of the "five-story hotel" got wind of it early, and more than 200 cell phones were found lying around on the upper yard near the MAC shack, while the goon squad found 100 more in cells. That is 300-plus phones that go for $300 to $500 a piece. Prisons are busy market places.

Not that long ago, two guards in the Adjustment Center, of all places,[1] were found to have many thousands of dollars worth of all kinds of dope stashed in their clothing lockers right there in the AC. They were caught red-handed. Sad for everyone. Two young men, with families, would spend many years in prison themselves, and they would have to be specially housed to keep them alive. The threat to their lives would no doubt come from the prison gangs that "hired" them.

Gangs operate in prison, although the CDRC makes every effort to control them.[2] On the lower yard, where the baseball field is, it is not so much that there are actual gangs, but by race or ethnicity convicts gather in areas that are defined by tables, benches, pull-up bars, and a couple hundred square feet of turf. People from other groups do not walk through another group's area without permission, and this goes for me, too.

If anyone from the California State Prison system reads this, they will not be shocked, and I am not trying to embarrass them. Prisons are wonderful in the sense that the people who are there, with rare exceptions, are best kept there. Our streets would not be safe without prisons. Unhappily, prison is a growth industry, because as the drug culture expands when marijuana is legalized, we will need even more prisons. I think criminology might be a good major for college students, as there will likely be some good career opportunities in that arena.

---

1   The Adjustment Center is a prison within a prison where the most dangerous cons are housed, but usually for only a relatively brief period. One would think that it would be a drug free zone.
2   Gangs or a "car" could be any grouping of people. A car is a group who share an identity, maybe even the chapel guys or the baseball team. Very important to have a car at your back; without it, a con is considered vulnerable to a whole host of nasty things.

Drugs in Prison   59

Opening Day 2010 season.

Here the prison's color guard, composed of ex-military, put on a good show.

15
Women at San Quentin

Over a century ago, women were housed at San Quentin in a brick building that extended east toward San Francisco Bay from the Count Gate, which is the main entrance into the prison. That ended in the 1920s, and since then the only women inside are correctional officers, state employees, volunteers, and lawyers. Of course, there are also visitors—wives, mothers, girlfriends, and daughters of the convicts.

Convicts can be very popular with certain women. The more notorious the crime the more sought after is the criminal. I know, this sounds strange.

Marriages take place from time to time. Mainline guys have the hope of a conjugal visit, which is a super big goal of many.[1] Pen pal clubs are like gold to convicts, and it is in this way that many find wives. Marriages are rarely consummated, though; some women divorce their men once they are released on parole. It is too complex for me to figure out, and I have engaged in many conversations with prisoners over the years about the reasons why.

State employees and volunteers will marry convicts after they are released, but the romance and maybe a little more starts behind the walls. For some ladies, a prison is a target-rich environment. Convicts are not real picky, it turns out, and rather bizarre pairings take place. Convicts have been known to take advantage of a woman who is desperate for a little love in her life and who can get talked into bringing stuff into the prison which she ought not.

Homosexuals find the prison a target-rich place as well—usually older men looking for a younger partner. It makes a certain amount of sense. Life is tough, and opportunities for a decent life are few for a convicted felon. Prison can be a safe haven—shelter, food, medical care, lots of entertainment of a sort, and people to take advantage of and not get arrested for doing it.

---

1   Years prior to the publication of this book, conjugal visits ceased.

Prison is a career choice for a number of folks.

At the beginning of my coaching at SQ, I was approached by some of the players who begged me to try to do something about a cop, a big strong and aggressive guard, who routinely molested vulnerable cons—the old, sick, disabled, and young. I eventually wrote an anonymous letter to the CDRC in Sacramento and pretended I was a parolee and wanted them to know about this dirt bag at Q. After some months, the predator cop disappeared, but we learned later on that he was merely transferred to Old Folsom. This, of course, is not a whole lot different from what goes on in some churches, except that the goings on in the prison system are rarely broadcast. And, I might add, given the enormous power and influence of the correctional officer's union, the whole thing will likely not see the light of day.

There is one female cop who often is assigned to the lower yard, which is where the baseball field is, who is friendly and well liked by the cons. She is in her mid thirties, attractive and outgoing. She will flash a smile and even touch convicts on the arm. That could be dangerous, but she is able to pull it off without creating a hormone storm, although her uniform pants are tighter than most, and it is obvious she has something going up top, too. Not a Hollywood face, but nice; it is the smile that is her best feature. Funny, I have never heard any rumors about her, and if there were any hanky panky going on, it would be all over.

During games, as part of doing her job, she will check out the baseball action. I have seen her standing amongst a bunch of convicts not far from the Giants dugout. Behind her would be two outdoor toilets, two to take care of number one and two to take care of number two, actually one unit, and she is careful to have her back to them.[2]

When she is intently watching a game, I notice some of the cons standing back and looking at her back side. One day several fans were studying the lady's charms, and I felt compelled to break up the party a little. Nothing was said, but it was at least a reality check. Frankly, I prefer that women would not place themselves in such a position, and I think a majority of the

---

2   Some years back the union pushed through the CDRC that female guards could be stationed in the cell blocks, which meant that, because the guard stations were always positioned close to where the convicts took showers, it would be impossible for a naked convict to escape being seen by a woman. Some may know what a "circle jerk" is, and a version of the same can take place. Some cons hate it that their dignity, what might be left of it, is denied; some love it, though, as indicated above.

cons would say the same.

It is said that everything that goes on in a prison has to do with sex. Perhaps I am naïve and don't see it. The guys who have been down a number of years don't want to get caught up in it, even the fantasy part. A mature con will just know that one of the losses he has is sex. Of course, there are plenty of guys who cannot control their hormones, and there is a certain homosexual population. I have heard it said that it really isn't homosexuality so much as an overpowering need for sex. It is all over my head, and for the most part I ignore the issue.

Convicts can be very careful to protect women at the prison. One famous story has it that one stormy evening a woman was teaching a class in the basement of the old educational building, when the power failed and all went dark. There was the sound of chairs being moved around but then silence. In a short while the lights came back on and there the convicts were, backs to the teacher encircling her with their arms interlocked. I am reasonably assured that it is a true story.

Opening Day 2010, Laura Bowman is given a game ball in appreciation for all she does for the sports programs at the prison. She clears into the prison the members of all the teams, including the baseball teams. It is no simple process.

16
Last Practice before Opening Day

Not anticipating any surprises, I had prepared the line-up for the upcoming game to be read out at the last practice before opening day—April 14, the day before Tax Day, which would not mean anything to the Giants, since none of them would be paying any taxes.

It is usual for me to announce the starters and their positions; it gives them a few days to prepare themselves mentally to play in front of the largest audience they will see all year. Plus, there will be members of the media present, and we take the time to discuss how and how not to be interviewed. In the past, a few guys had gotten political, which got back to the warden.

The real reason for the pre-game briefing is for those who thought they would be or ought to be on the starting team to get the disappointment out of their systems before game time. Chemistry is the whole thing. A sulking, angry, complaining team member can make a bad day out of what should be a high experience for everyone. But, as it turned out, my line-up card had to be torn up, since our first baseman and number four hitter had gone on the disabled list with severe back trouble.

When my old friends and I get together and look back on our ball playing days, we don't recall the score of the game or few of the details of what happened. What we remember is the fun we had.

After the meeting at the mound, we practiced pick-off moves to first with a runner on first base, then a special move to first with a runner on both first and second started by a verbal sign from the third baseman. Not a very efficient practice, but a necessary one. Once the pitchers rotated through the drill, we went to practicing run downs, another time-consuming but necessary drill. The coaching staff is embarrassed when a rundown goes awry.

Next, the starters took infield and outfield—I call it "in and out"—and final instructions were given about how the ball is thrown around the infield following an out with no runners on base. Simple stuff, but if not rehearsed until it is done right, the team, not to mention the coaches, are going to look unprepared and sloppy. Following the starters, the back-ups took the field and even looked better, which was not lost on them.

Four baseballs were signed, so they would be ready for giving to the dignitaries, such as the warden, as part of the opening day ceremonies. Chris Rich had prepared a document with all the players, coaches, umpires, scorekeepers, equipment and ground keepers listed, with a way to keep score. He had even researched the history of baseball at the prison and included that.

The sun sank below the wall in right field and took away the light we needed to defend ourselves from line drives and wild pitches as the batting practice reached its conclusion. Dave Baker, our team chaplain—not elected but appointed by me—sat down with me to discuss a delicate issue as the equipment and field-working tools were collected to be deposited in the green sheet metal boxes we used to store our gear. It had come to our attention that not all the players enjoyed the short testimony and shorter prayer Dave led at the conclusion of the games. Also, some thought the visiting teams were sort of trapped into participation, and that some would, if given the chance, opt out. In a quick minute Dave and I agreed we would announce our intent when we invited anyone who wanted to, to join us out at the mound. We will see in two days whether this will satisfy or not.

Opening Day 2010 Pre-game Talk

17
Opening Day

Saturday, April 17, game time 10:30 a.m.
The threat of rain vanished by Wednesday, which rid me of one worry. Now there remained a possible lock-down at the prison or a computer glitch. This second thing, a computer glitch, would mean that the incoming team, Elliot Smith's Cubs/Oaks, would not be cleared in. Though neither trouble had ever impacted an opening day, many other games had been lost due to one or the other over the years.

The new warden, Vincent S. Cullen, would throw out the first pitch. He had already earned a reputation of being tough but fair. I was told he had been practicing his pitch to the plate. Then there would be the media. My favorite sportswriter for the San Francisco Chronicle, Scott Ostler, would be there with a staff photographer, Paul Chen. For the last several seasons I had emailed an invitation to our Opening Day, and this time Scott got the go ahead from the managing editor. Then the LA Times would be there as well as a crew from KQED. (The KQED crew turned out to be two young women who got a whole lot of attention.)

My old high school buddy, Bill Mauck, was coming down from Redding to take photos, which he had done before. Two church members, Carl Laur and Jim Parker, who work with me on our television program, would also be there working with cameras, and my wife Katie would have our new little Nikon camera. (In total, we would be processing about eight hundred images.)

Katie, Bill, Jim, Carl, and I were the first outside people to get down to the lower yard, and we were happy to see the "Field of Dreams" striped, or chalked, the infield dirt smoothed and ready, and uniformed players playing catch in left field. What a relief.

Our starting first baseman and number four hitter, Redd Casey, had been on crutches just three days prior due to a pinched nerve in his back. Usually, I have the line-up card ready to go, but this time I had to wait until

I knew if Redd would be ready to go or not. Soon as I got close enough, I scanned the outfield looking for number 8, and sure enough, there he was. I immediately walked to the dugout and filled out the card.

San Quentin Giants' 2010 opening day would probably not be described as a spectacle. But for us—the players, coaches, and even the correctional officers, warden's office, and others, even some in the general convict population—it was a proud day. As soon as I saw that the warden had arrived, accompanied by Lt. Rudy Luna, Lt. Sam Robinson, Laura Bowman, and Don DeNevi, the Giants lined up along the 3rd base line, and the visiting team, Elliot's Cubs/Oaks lined up along the first base line. Down the right field line was a color guard with flags, one the US and the other the State of California. This was put together, as it is every year, by the Vietnam Veterans Group of San Quentin (VVGSQ). Our head grounds crewman, Willie, is also a member of this group. The veterans marched smartly in, wheeled around behind home plate, stepped quickly toward the pitcher's mound, did an about face, and presented colors. Drew Schroller, our score keeper, much to my surprise, walked out and sang the National Anthem, without accompaniment, and did a very fine job.

The Color Guard

Observing the American tradition, the VFW group makes this happen.

At the very end, at the part, "over the land of the free" everyone started clapping and yelling—just like at a San Francisco Giants game. There was no fly over.

Now it was up to me to make presentations. After a brief speech, and forgetting to introduce our hard-working coaches, Kevin Loughlin, Mike Deeble, Stan Damas, and Elliot Smith, I became a politician of sorts. Before the game, eight baseballs had been signed by the team, and one by one I handed them out—to the dignitaries—the last one going to the warden after he made the toss to our catcher, Johnny Taylor.

Game time had finally arrived, and we were more than ready. One last huddle up, during which I once again delivered my now infamous line, "See the ball, catch the ball; see the ball, hit the ball." Then, "one, two, three, Giants" and the team took the field.

2010 Opening Day Lineup

Giants along the third base line and the Cubs/Colts along the first, Color Guard in the middle.

Left:

Drew Schroller singing the national anthem.

Warden Cullen

Ready to throw out the first pitch.

Opening Day   69

Left:

Kent gives a speech on Opening Day: April 17, 2010.

Right:

Warden Vincent S. Cullen on the left and Lt. Sam Robinson on the right.

Right:

Willie and Nick

Left:

Coach Kevin Loughlin

18
More Opening Day

The Visiting Team Coming in to Play the San Quentin Giants

The Cubs/Oaks—two old guys, Elliot and Jim, both in their sixties, while the rest of the team is composed of players in their twenties and thirties. None had been professional ball players, but they knew the game and had played it for years in various leagues in the Bay Area. They were serious, as we say, *hard-nosed* guys, who played to win.

    The Cubs/Oaks starter threw hard, and the Giants simply could not get going. We had few base runners, which severely cut into my small-ball type of game with stealing, hit and run, pickles, squeezes, and especially bunting. Only one time did I give a steal sign and not one hit and run or squeeze. Instead, we hit five doubles and two home runs.

Our defense was sharp except for two innings, during which we gave the game away. Same old thing—trying to make two plays at the same time. "See the ball, catch the ball" did not work. Twice, in double play situations, an eye was taken off the ball into the glove in order to check on the runner coming to second base. Instead of at least one out, the grounder ended up in an outfielder's glove.

The slide began, however, when our center fielder lost sight of an easy fly ball. There is a towering wall painted light yellow just behind home plate, and Terry Burton could not pick the ball up. Trouble was that the bases were loaded. Something like seven runs scored in the inning, and we never did catch up.

Around the sixth inning, I was frustrated, and unhappily, I unconsciously let it show. Our outfield play had been passive—instead of charging a ball with runners on base, our guys were overly cautious, making weak throws to the cut-off man. All the while, runners were running around the bases scoring runs. I called the outfielders over as they were heading into the dugout and got on them about their lack of aggressiveness. Their down cast faces told me to leave that approach behind and go to an encouragement mode instead. It was an event that lasted less than a minute but will stay with me awhile.

Front Shot Cubs/Oaks Coming In

Going into the last of the ninth, the Giants were behind 16 to 5. The young, pretty KQED ladies were still there, the reporters were filling up notebooks, and the photographers were snapping away. The warden and other prison officials had hung on, and there we were, losing badly on opening day. I overheard some talk about when was the last time the local nine had lost on opening day. No one could remember so far back.

In the bottom of the ninth, the Giants came alive. Five runs scored quickly, and with only one out, we were six runs down and had two men on base. But that would be the end of it. Everyone saw, however, that we did not quit, and Scott Ostler, the sports reporter for the *San Francisco Chronicle*, would comment in his article on the game that appeared in the paper April 19, that "Nobody has to remind these guys that you can't win 'em all."

Before the game started, I was warned by our coach and my old friend, Stan Damas, that the opposing team did not want to be part of the closing prayer on the mound following the end of the game. I nodded to Stan and said I understood. It had already been made plain that some of the Giants and coaching staff did not want to be on the mound either. Dave Baker, our team chaplain, and I had discussed this but were going ahead anyway on an invitational type of basis.

Scott Ostler Interviews Chris Rich

There we were on the mound. I looked around and saw almost the entire Giants team present. More than that, I saw also nearly the entire visiting team there, too. I gave my little speech, coach type speech, and Dave took over. He announced there would be a prayer and if someone did not want to be there, that was fine. He paused. No one moved.

What a fine gentleman Dave is. During the game he had been to plate only once and did not make it through the one inning he was pitching. But you would not have known he had been through a tough time on the field.

After a brief comment or two, he offered a short prayer and thanked the visitors for coming in.

The Giants gathered one more time, got into a huddle, extended our right arms into the air to touch in the middle and "one, two, three, Giants" echoed across the prison, bouncing off the cell block walls. I thought I saw a tear or two in the eyes of some of the players.

Above:

Dominique Interviewed by a KQED Reporter

A Second KQED Reporter

19

Dishon

Of the last three scheduled games we lost one and had two cancelled. It was not unusual to have games cancelled. San Quentin, after all, is a prison, and the warden's priorities are not always in sync with what the ball players hope for.

This time, the loss was to a team we should have rolled over easily. The opposing team's starter threw in the 50s, speed wise, and I would have loved to have hit against him myself. Without the walks he handed us, we would not have scored the two runs we did squeak out with our three-hit attack. Too much softball is my thought. Convicts play a lot of slow-pitch softball, and it tweaks their swings to the extreme. The softball is an easier target than a baseball, comes in slow, and the uppercut swings work for slow pitch but not often for baseball.

Two weeks previous, during the beginning of a game, Dishon had shown up, asking for a chance to make the team as a pitcher. In his twenties somewhere, black, missing front teeth, baggy pants with no belt, with a scraggly beard making me wonder if he was Muslim, I did not think he looked much like a ball player. I told him to come back next game, as I had no time to even talk to him. He nodded and drifted away, but right in the middle of the game he tried to walk in and sit down on the bench. Before he walked past me, I stopped him and told him he could not sit in the dugout. He nodded, said he was sorry, and left. Next game he approached me again and asked to try out. I spent a few minutes explaining that we already had too many players, who had been working out for months, and there was no chance, unless he was a phenom. He heard me, nodded, and walked away, except that he hung close by and cheered the team on during the game.

Toward the close of the game, I called him over and asked him about his baseball experience. He said he played in high school and college but under questioning he was somewhat vague about the details. In any case, I recruited a bench player to take Dishon down to the bull pen and find out what he could do. A couple of times I glanced out toward the bull pen to see what I could see. Very average at best was my estimation. After the game he wanted to talk, and I told him I doubted he would even be able to practice with the team. He walked away and only said, "Okay, coach."

Next game he was back. I had some time before the game and fished an outfielder's glove out of my equipment bag, and we walked down to the bull pen. I wanted to see for myself. We played some catch before I asked him to pitch out of a wind up and then out of the stretch. What he showed me merely confirmed that he was less than an average player and certainly no phenom. I had to tell him what I thought. He countered with a request to be able to practice with the team so he could show me what he could do, but I said no.

That game and the game after, Dishon was the team's most enthusiastic fan. He made it a point to stand right by the dugout and yell encouragement to the players. Twice I had to call him over and explain that we did not coach from the side lines, since it would be a distraction and not a help. He quickly assented to this and still hung close by with words of "well done" to the players.

Dishon

Later that evening I reflected on how the Giants players were reacting to Dishon. In times past, if someone was hanging on trying to be on the team, the players themselves would find ways to discourage the man. In the case of Dishon, they were not doing this; in fact, there was an unspoken acceptance apparent. But I did not want him on the team. Based on what I had seen of his athletic skills, he would merely sit on the bench along with a dozen others not in the starting lineup.

Before the May 1 game, the three-hit game against a poor team, I was informed that Willie, the Vietnam vet and our grounds keeper, had suffered a heart attack and would not likely be able to continue working on the field. Toward the middle of the game, most of it with Dishon at what had become his post right next to the dugout and therefore right next to me cheering the team on, I had a thought. Dishon take Willie's place? I talked to Frankie, our inmate coach, and Kevin Loughlin, who was running that game, about the idea, and they both said it sounded like a good idea.

After the game I drew Dishon aside and asked him if he wanted the job. He stared at me for a moment and nodded yes. We shook hands, and then I added, "Dishon, the workman is worthy of his hire (right out of the Bible), and you will be able to practice now with the team."

"Okay, coach."

Giants Dugout along the Third Base Line

20
I Did the Best I Could, Coach!

The title for this chapter came from Dave Baker after a game that will not be easily forgotten. But we will look at that story a bit later. Right now, we go back to May 8 and do some updating.

Saturday, the 8th of May, we played Sting, mostly young guys, and we started the pitcher we thought had the best chance of winning the game—Matt White. His arm was not quite ready, but he wanted the ball anyway. Kevin Loughlin was running the game and making the calls at third. I was helping out with the details—bench coach would be the job title. Matt ran into trouble early, gave up a flock of runs, and rubbing his arm came out of the game. What followed did not help much, but the Giants rallied some in the last couple of innings, and at least we got into the double digits, though a loss, 17 to 11. Mario Ellis hit a home run—the only highlight.

Dishon, now helping with field maintenance, hung around the dugout the whole game, and I gave him one of my gloves to play catch. At one point, I worked with him on his swing and bunting. A strong young man, and though he had the typical prison-house softball swing, it looked like there was some hope.

There was something about Dishon I liked. Whether he was just conning me I could not tell for sure. My guess was he had grown up without a father, never had any money or chances for any, and had done what so many did—sell dope to get a slice of the American dream. After an arrest and conviction or two, his chances were gone. This is what I thought; I never really did talk to him about his life to find out.

On May 12, a Wednesday, the Giants played the Oaks/Cubs again, Elliot Smith's team that had beaten us opening day. Mario pitched and did well, but by the end of four the score was 4 to 3, the Giants with the 3. Frankie Smith, an inmate, was running the game from third. Normally he coaches first, but I like to have our coaches manage games, and Frankie and Chris count as coaches. (Chris is currently trying to rehab his knee on which he had surgery only a week ago, and soon he will get to call a game and maybe even pitch down the road. He has won more games as a starter than any other pitcher in San Quentin's history, I am quite sure, but I would really like to use him as a closer to save his knee.)

At the end of the fourth I had to leave. For two days I had been battling a cold, but it got the better of me, so I didn't get to see the end of the game. The next day Kevin sent me a text saying that Redd Casey, our first baseman and clean-up hitter, who had not done a thing for an unreasonably long time for Redd, lofted a walk-off two run shot over the right field fence when we were down to our last at bat. Mario got the win, having gone the distance. A great win for Frankie, his first.

Dishon had been in uniform for this game, and I introduced him as a new member of the team prior to the start of play. He did not get in the game, but he was pleased to be a Giant. He functioned as bat boy, scurrying around the dugout doing what he could to help.

Then Saturday, May 15, we played the All Blacks, whom we had beaten April 24, with Henry getting the win. Kevin would be running the game up until he had to leave to catch a flight back East, and I would then take over. By this time my cold was almost gone, and I was ready to manage a game, which I hadn't done since April 24. By the way, there is not one black man on the All blacks; the whole reference is they wear black uniforms.

Their starting pitcher—how do I politely describe him? His fast ball could not have reached fifty miles an hour. He had no breaking pitch or anything else. All the hitters saw was a white beach ball lofting toward them and try as they might, not a solid hit was made until the third inning. How embarrassing—yes, embarrassing. Coaches under such circumstances are embarrassed; maybe ashamed is a better word, because in some way they must accept the responsibility for the awful play. But the pitcher, not a young man, not athletic looking at all, somehow managed to get outs. He would have been well suited for the before picture in a weight-loss ad. It was actually worse than that, but decorum restrains me.

Kevin departed in the bottom of the sixth inning, leaving me with the game. Right away, and of course due to nothing I was doing, we got a couple of runners on base. I started doing my tricks—stealing, bunting, pickles—stuff I learned from being a fan of Tony LaRussa, my favorite big-league manager over the years. Yes, I admit it; I will call for a suicide squeeze with two outs in the inning and two strikes on the hitter. And yes, I will say that so far I have never had that play backfire.

Let me brag just a bit, because I did something I had never done before. Close to the end of the game, there were two outs and a runner on second and third. We were ahead by one run, but I was desperate for another. As though scripted from above, an alarm sounded, and all the convicts had to sit down right where they were. Free people do not have to do so, giving me time to trot out to second and talk to none other than Dishon who was on second base, having just gotten his first hit as a Giant, a solid double with a run batted in. I told him that if the next hitter was down by two strikes, I wanted him to casually wander so far off second that he would draw the attention of the pitcher. Now the pitcher was their closer and a savvy player, but like I said, I was desperate. I wanted Dishon to get into a pickle. Usually, a pickle is set up with a man on first and third each, but this was going to be different. I told Dishon to get hung up long enough so that we could score the runner on third. If the runner on third crossed home plate before Dishon was tagged out, the run would count, and we would be two runs up.

Dishon could not have done it better. The runner on third hugged the bag initially, as I asked him to, then charged a little down the line and stopped. Dishon now broke for third. That was enough for the pitcher, who was running hard at Dishon with the ball held high in his throwing hand, just like the book says to do, but it was too late. Our runner, I do not remember his name, streaked like crazy for home and slid in for the run— which I thought would be more than enough to win the game.

Kevin Driscoll had started the game, ran out of gas, then Chris had come in with the bases loaded and two outs and got the third out.

Dave Baker

Chris was wearing a brace on his repaired knee, and perhaps it was a dumb thing to do, but Chris said he was ready, and I was, again like I said, desperate, so I let him go in. Kevin Loughlin, now gone, probably would not have let Chris in the game, as he is usually more cautious than I am.

Chris wanted to pitch the next inning as well, and as I was desperate, I said yes. He got an out, then walked one, hit one, got a ground ball for an out, walked another, and the big guy, the starting pitcher was up with the bases loaded. He had not done a thing all game, and I was beginning to think all my hair would turn gray that game. Chris had him two and two, and probably not wanting to pitch to even the big guy with a full count, laid one out over the plate, and bang, a grand slam. It was a crusher, not a sound; I couldn't look at Chris and see the pain he would be in. He got the next hitter, but now we were down two runs with three needed to win.

But we got even, then we went up by two. Now Dave Baker was pitching. Dave's baseball skills had declined remarkably since the last season. I should have explained at the outset that due to a lock-down of one dorm in H Unit, two pitchers, Matt and Henry, could not come up to the Lower Yard. Matt was supposed to have started the game. There was only Rico and Dave available, and Rico only lasted 1/3 of an inning before I had to remove him and bring in Dave. Dave managed to get out of that inning, but the next one he hit two batters, walked three and before we could realize it, our lead had evaporated and we were down two runs.[1]

Last of the ninth we squeaked out a run but with two outs, Mike Tyler, our fastest player, got thrown out at second trying to steal, and the game ended with a Giants loss, 14 to 13. I was so depressed, I did not even line up for the high five stuff. Instead, I went over to Coach, the head of the umpire "union" and complained about poor positioning of the umpires which resulted in missing the call on Mike's steal attempt.

There was no team meeting, no one, two, three, Giants. After I vented, I went to the dugout and started to get my cleats off. Sitting a couple yards away was Dave. He looked at me and simply said, "I did the best I could, coach."

"I know you did," was all I could say. But it was true; Dave had done the best he could.

---

[1] One day while I was coaching at third base, Dave was at the plate and hit a line drive at me which I could not dodge. Loud crack, and I fell to the ground. Next thing I knew, the prison ambulance was right there, with the players huddled around me. Asked if I was okay, I said no. After a while, I got up and continued coaching at third.

On the drive home I thought about those words, "I did the best I could." It is usually the case that we do the best we can, but the best is often not enough and in more of life than just ball games. Dave had committed murder, had a fifteen to life sentence, and due to California politics understood that he would have to spend another dozen or more years on top of the seventeen he had already done. He was married with children, and desperately wanted to go home. His playing days were flying by, his hair was turning gray—he was visibly aging. Perhaps he thought that he might have played in his last game.

Left:

Kevin Driscoll:
Pitcher, 3rd Base, and Hitter

Right:

Matt White:
Pitcher

I Did the Best I Could, Coach!

Above and Left:

**Redd Casey:
Home Run Hitter and 1st Base**

Right:

**Mario Ellis:
Short Stop and Pitcher**

21
Four Sqeezes

The Redwood Empire League Titans team of 2009 became the REBL, or Rebel Giants this year, a thirty-eight-and-over team. No real standouts, but a solid team, nevertheless. They pitch, hit, and field—seasoned ball players.

Wednesday evening, May 19, we got a late start, mostly due to me. First, the correctional officer in charge of North Block where most of the team members reside would not give an early release to the ball players. But second was that I had forgotten that Kevin was out of town and would not be bringing in the outside team, the Giants. By the time we got started we would be fortunate to get in five innings.

Added to that, H Unit was locked down, and every one of the players there were starters in the game, so the lineup I had prepared was useless. I was visibly frustrated, so much so that Frankie asked me what was wrong, and when I gave him a gruff answer, he wanted to know if I wanted to talk about it. I'm sorry for it now, but I turned him down.

Since Kevin Driscoll would have to start Saturday's game, May 22, that left me with Dave, Terry, and Rico—one would have to start on the mound. I went with Dave. The first inning was his worst; he gave up one run and left two on base. However, he did not walk or hit anyone. He was making the REBL Giants hit the ball and they did. Then he reeled off four more innings of scoreless ball. Behind him the team made some excellent plays, including a spectacular one by Lamarr at short.

However, my Giants were not hitting at all. Softball swings lofted pop-ups, several were caught looking at third strikes, and even bunt attempts were going awry. At the end of five, it was 1 to nothing—the Giants owned the nothing. It was almost time for the yard to be closed, when everyone must head back to their cells. We lined up and were preparing to do the high five closure when Chris Rich, otherwise known as Stretch, yelled out that we might have time for one more inning if we hurried.

We hurried. I had taken Dave out of the game in the last of the fifth for a pinch hitter, so Terry Burton rushed out to the mound, took five or less warm-up throws, and proceeded, in five pitches, to shut the REBL Giants down in the top of the sixth.

In the bottom of the inning, our first batter hit a weak ground ball back to the pitcher. One out. Time left—5 minutes or less.

James Bautista, playing second as usual and leading off, pushed a bunt past the pitcher and the first baseman came off the bag to field it, but the second baseman did not get to first in time to receive the throw. A man on—a fast man on.

James Bautista

I gave James the steal sign on the first pitch. He got the same sign on the second pitch and now was on third. On the third pitch the batter got a suicide squeeze sign, laid it down, and James scored easily. Now there were two outs and no one on base, but the game was tied, one to one.

Squeezes are of two types, safety and suicide. The safety squeeze is when the runner on third does not commit to home plate until the batter bunts the ball and hits the dirt. This is so in case the batter fails to bunt the ball on the ground, then the runner can get back to the third base bag. Earlier in the game I had tried two safety squeezes, both of which had failed. The second squeeze is the suicide variety, and this is where the runner breaks for the plate as soon as the pitcher has clearly committed to throw to the catcher. If the hitter does not get the bat on the ball, the runner is dead, that is, dead out—so suicide squeeze.

One suicide squeeze had worked; now we needed a runner. The next batter, our short stop, Lamarr King, was not hitting at all, so Johnny, our injured catcher, hit for him. He managed to roll a ball between first and second base, and when both infielders went for it, Johnny had a weird sort of hit.

Prior to the beginning of the inning, I'd asked two of our bench players, not the best ball players but very fast guys, to heat up—Mike Tyler and Charles Lyons. Now I needed one of them, and as I walked toward the dugout from the third base coaching box, I was trying to decide who it would be. A couple of games before, Mike had pinch ran and did not get a good jump off first, so I went with Charles.

Time out! Johnny came out and Charles went to first. I spoke to him while he was finding a batting helmet and told him to steal second on the very first pitch. Then once there he was going to get a suicide squeeze sign. I told the hitter the plan as Charles trotted down to first base.

The whole team saw the crazy thing I was doing, and the dugout went into freeze frame mode—all was silent; no one moved. They knew I could call for a squeeze with two outs and even two strikes on the hitter, which I had done once in the game already—but this was almost beyond the beyond. I thought so, too, but I knew that we had only one minute to go before the lower yard officer called the game so the Close B guys could be counted. To fool around with that, and send the guys up late, might mean they would no longer be allowed to be on the team at all. The risk had to be taken; there would be a squeeze.

Charles Lyons

Now Charles is the fastest man in San Quentin, or at least I had been told this. His job was to get a good lead, hit the third base bag and keep going. No stopping, no looking, just run. Stafont Smith, playing third base for us, was at bat. He laid down a bunt; it rolled about eight feet in front of home plate and the catcher charged out to make the play. He made a clean grab of the ball but had to hesitate because the first baseman had also charged the bunt. Too late, the throw was high anyway, and Charles was almost at the plate. He would not have had to slide but he did; a big, grand belly flop on the plate, lots of dust.

This was the first real contribution Charles had been able to make to the team all year. A young black man, shy and quiet, he was nearly beside himself with joy. He got a huge reception from the team just feet from home plate. We were all glad to see Charles do well. Then the high fives began. The other team took it well; in fact, they were stunned by what happened, and I had to listen to lots of praise from both teams for the squeeze calls. Making calls—you can look like a genius or a jerk. Now I was a hero, but in the next game, I could be the other.

Left:

Umpires Nick and Coach McSween

Below:

Umpire Will

22
Roofs

Saturday, May 22nd, with the Giants playing the Tigers, mostly young players, three of whom had played college ball. The lead went back and forth. Both teams alternately played well and poorly.

Because two of our starting pitchers missed their turns due to an H Unit lock down, the reason for which I will describe in a moment, the coaching staff thought it best to give each of our three starters some innings. Matt pitched the first three, Kevin the second set, and Mario finished up.

But back to the reason for the lock down in H Unit. H Unit is a dorm set up with bunk beds, about 250 men per dorm, for a total of about one thousand convicts, as there are four units. These men have gotten their "number" down to the point that the custody requirements are reduced. Many will go home within a fairly short time, some in just months, others in a year or two. Lifers are housed in North Block.

The convicts from H Unit were allowed to go to the lower yard on Monday the 17th of May, a rainy day, but the rain did not begin in earnest until the yard was full of convicts. The correctional officers unwisely took shelter in a little shack on the yard and were not paying close attention to what the convicts were doing. The story I heard was that some men, out of frustration for having to stand in the rain for a few hours, decided to invade a double wide mobile structure that was used for classrooms. They had access to it through an opening in the centerfield fence. At one point, there had been a gate in place with padlock, and there now is again, but that day, the convicts merely walked through and broke into the first classroom. They proceeded to vandalize, steal, urinate, and defecate their way through both classrooms, making their way from one classroom to the other by going through the ceiling and then down through the roof of the second classroom. Undiscovered, the convicts made their way back to H Unit. An officer eventually discovered the mischief, and the prison came abuzz. One of the deputy wardens went down to the dorm in H Unit where the culprits were known to be housed, and in the midst of his reprimand, the convicts treated him so terribly with their name calling and taunting that he shut the whole place down.

Jumping now right to the end of the game—we went into the last of the ninth down 8 to 6. We scored one run with a walk, a steal, and a hit. With one out and no one on base, we got a runner on due to an error. The next hitter struck out, and we were down to Lamarr King, the former phenom, at the plate.

Lamarr had not started and had been moping around the dugout, maybe trying to show how upset he was at not starting. He did not start, since Mario was at short. But when Mario went to the mound to start the seventh inning, Lamarr was inserted at short. His first at bat looked awful, much the same as he had looked the last couple of games. Here he was, though—not the guy I wanted to have up.

First pitch, a terrible swing at a fast ball right down broadway. The same with the second pitch. Count—0 and 2. One more pitch, I figured, and game over. The third pitch, same exact place, thigh high, fast ball right across the heart of the plate, and Lamarr got all of it, a towering drive that easily cleared the fence and landed on the roof—yes, the roof of that very classroom building.

Again, just like on TV, a big reception at home plate. I was hoping Lamarr's success would turn him around. There he was, the hero of the game.

Few moments of baseball at San Quentin are like the aftermath of a surprise and dramatic win like we experienced with Lamarr's homer. We did not want to leave the field. A sudden thought struck me, however—here we were jumping around hugging each other—could this be considered over-familiarity?

Over-familiarity—we were warned against such when we took the training to receive a brown card. This card, the size of a driver's license, meant the possessor could come into the prison, go down to the Lower Yard without an escort, and could even escort others, like outside baseball players, into the prison. Now I was worried that all the commotion and emotions being displayed among the players and coaches might be considered inappropriate. As best I could, after I caught on to the issue, I tried to calm things down.

Sticking to the rules has stunted many a happy time on the ball yard for me. I knew about the ever-watchful eye of the guards in the gun towers. And a report would be made, too. We had gotten away with plenty already.

Dave brought us all out to the mound; he invited anyone who wanted to be part of the prayer to join in or not. Most stayed.

Two double plays with Lamarr firing to first base.

23

The Experiment

Before the tryouts in February, our coaches decided we did not want certain players, despite playing skills, on the Giants. It was a step I had wanted to make for some time. As any coach knows, having discontented players moping around the dugout is, at minimum, bad chemistry. We made the move knowing there would be consequences of some sort.

Within a short time, these malcontented players formed a kind of lobby and pressured the prison officials to have a second team. (It has surprised me on more than one occasion how much clout prisoners can have.) There were phone calls and meetings, and eventually it was agreed that those convicts who wanted to play baseball could form an intramural team. They would get the field every other Monday night and every Saturday night. Plus, they would have access to our equipment. But—and this was a major item for me—they would not play outside teams.

It was agreed—intramural baseball it would be, and we would share bats, balls, gloves, and so on.

Little by little new demands were made. The No Name[1] team wanted to play the Giants. They wanted uniforms. They wanted to play outside teams. The original contract allowed for none of these.

The pressure was on again. Behind my back some of the convicts who had not made the Giant's roster had been selling their "needs" to someone who might be able to make it happen, and when I found out, I knew I had to make a stand one way or another.

Little by little, I began to talk to some of the leaders on the upstart team. I listened and tried to understand what they were hoping to do. Perhaps, I thought, if I made more accommodations things could be worked out. For some time, the talks went on; I began to wonder if I could not stall until the season was over. That thought was quickly followed by a guilty feel-

---

1   This designation came late. Early on it was Poison, Cancer, Upstart, or Rebel.

ing. After all, they only wanted to play baseball, and here I was, in a place of power and authority, sort of, denying these poor guys some fun in the sun.

But then there was the Willing[2], my old "outside" team, and some of the guys who had played in years past along with some new players were contacting me about having some games with the Giants. Three of these were young men whom I had coached at Tam High in Mill Valley as freshman—Alex Ritchie, Graham McKennee, Kyle Patrick—all pitchers. Alex was a senior and Graham and Kyle had been playing college ball.

Of course, I thought, two birds might be killed with one stone—have the Willing play the No Name team. Perfect. It would be an experiment, and I expressed it just that way to everyone at the prison—players on both teams, and to those who supervised me. I hinted that if things went well, who knew what good things might follow.

A game was set for May 24, a Monday night, a time slot the No Name team had as a practice time. It would be the Willing versus the No Name team, a real game.

When probed about the make-up of the Willing, I mentioned that Alex Ritchie and Graham McKennee threw in the high eighties. Brows furrowed and backs stiffened—No Name could not lose such a game, since it was to be a test, in more ways than one. It would be clear whether No Name was good enough to play more than intramural ball and whether the cast of characters on the team could behave themselves and be trusted to play outside teams. Positive results might mean a game with the Giants, which was really the chief goal. No Name players wanted to show they were better than the Giants players.

The day arrived, count cleared early, Officer Wood at the East Gate was cordial, the count gate officer was his same gruff, sarcastic self, and earlier than usual the teams were warming up, the field was being striped, the umpires put in an appearance, and the wind had died down some.

One particular convict had proved himself to be so awful at calling balls and strikes that I had loudly declared I would not manage a ball game if he were behind the plate. His strike zone was no bigger than the proverbial bread box, and he had the reputation of being inconsistent—calling plays in a favorable way for the team he wanted to win. The guy who organized the umpiring crew was nowhere in sight, contrary to his usual habit, and right away I began to wonder what was going on.

Alex started on the mound and could not get a strike call. He looked at me a couple of times and I shrugged my shoulders as if to say, I know,

---

[2] "Willing" meant those who were willing to come into a prison to play baseball.

I know, but there is nothing I can do. The game was fairly out of hand at the end of the second inning—walks and more walks. At the end of the first inning players tried to encourage Alex, and at the end of the second as well, and his last inning, the third—nothing much more could be said. Alex is a big young man, patient, so good natured, and he simply took it and did not react at all, even after the No Name pitcher plunked him with a pitch that looked for all the world to be done deliberately.

Graham came on to pitch in the fourth inning and threw hard strikes that had the umpire visibly worried the catcher might not stop the ball. Right down the middle, thigh high—ball, ball, ball. Graham grasped the situation and slowed his pitches, and some of the batters began to swing away. Despite this, and for the two innings Graham threw, no one touched the ball. Six strike outs, mixed in with walks which Graham could not help.

That was not all. The pitcher, the only pitcher the No Name team used, the worst of the poison guys, also plunked Graham. Then one of their runners, going from second to third on a ground ball, crashed into the short stop as he was positioned to receive the grounder and knocked him flat. Timothy McCall, playing short for the Willing, told me at the end of the game that his jaw was still numb from the forearm he'd received.

Graham got it the worst, though. On a steal attempt at home, when the ball skipped by the poor catcher who was trying to catch Graham's sliders, Graham came down from the mound to make the play and the runner crashed into him, the runner having failed, or something, to slide.

I guess I will also mention two outrageous calls the home plate ump made, yes that one, that were so awful it forced Len Zemarkowitz, who was sponsoring the No Name team and is a very good umpire in our county, to step up and reverse the calls, both of which would have gone against the Willing.

The game ended and high fives were exchanged, but I was engaged with an umpire who was trying to apologize for the terribly called game. We were joined by the convict player who had organized No Name in the beginning and had been largely responsible for putting the pressure on me. He knew what I was probably thinking, and I was not going to prove him wrong. To both of them I ended the conversation with, "Looks like the experiment worked. I have all the data I need."

Next Page: The Willing, May 24, 2010, in to play the No Name team for an experiment. Left to right: Tim McCall, Kevin Loughlin, Timothy McCall, Alex Baker, Bob McKennee, Alex Ritchie, Bill Baker, Graham McKennee, John Spilman, David Barker, Kent Philpott, Tucker Kuhn.

Below: The second photo was taken inside the prison and included Shane Kennedy, Alex Ritchie, Kevin Loughlin, a few players I'd coached at Tam High School, and one of their dads.

24
A Boycott

The inmate umpires below were working games in the late 1990s. They did the best they could, and I had a lot of fun teaching them the fine points. One of the guys pictured below was somewhat unreliable, seeing as he functioned as a kind of bookie and took wagers on the outcome of the games. We all knew but let it go, since we had little other choice.

I mentioned in the last chapter that following the Willing versus the No Name team, I had engaged one of the umpires in a discussion. Engage is not exactly the right word—I vented, and loudly—would be a more apt description. Okay, I try to remain calm and cool, but I am also a baseball guy, and I lost it a bit. Well, lost it is not exactly the right way to put it either. I was mad, and I might have sworn some, too. Gesturing over much, I stated that certain umpires, mainly the game's home plate ump, would not be behind the plate for any games I managed, ever again.

For the game on the 26th of May, the umpire crew did not show up, due to unknown reasons. We had to improvise, which worked, but I was told that the reason no umpires showed up is that there was a boycott of the games due to my behavior and demands.

This was not the first time, either. During the two previous seasons I had also been boycotted by the inmate umpires for several games. By not giving in, by finding others who were willing to umpire and risking the scorn of the other convicts, and by asking the outside teams to bring in an umpire or two, the boycott would end after a while. The prison runs on a principle that is easy to understand and one I accept—pay back. Not revenge, exactly, but there had to be a way the convicts could express their displeasure and frustration.

In previous years, after some talking and negotiating, the boycotts would end, and we would all put it behind us. This new boycott started on May 26, and for three games now—one with The Mission, one with Sting, and the last one, June 2, with The Willing, the boycott has continued, and there is an ominous sense present on the lower yard now. At this writing, June 3, after a series of wins and good baseball played by the Giants, I am not sure how things are going to turn out.

June 5 we play the Barons, and Frank deRosa, who heads the team, always brings in his own umpire, Nils Nielson, so not much of a problem. But I suspect that Nils will have to call the whole game by himself.

To resolve the differences there will have to be some conversations with the convict who organized the umpires some years ago. I could be unyielding and recruit other inmate umpires, assigning a couple of our Giants players each game on a rotating basis to officiate, and ask the outside teams to bring in at least one umpire for their games. I know, though, what will happen—there will be a whole lot of bad feelings, and some convicts will resent me for a long time. No volunteer has yet been harmed physically, which event would shut down a number of programs, but the real threat is having contraband planted in an equipment bag or rumors spread that I groped somebody. Something of this nature has been done before.

I don't like what is shaping up, and I am definitely not looking forward to Saturday's game. Maybe it is all just in my head.

25
An Update

The Giants' record is now 11 wins and 5 losses. I doubt that the 2008 record of 35 wins and 10 losses will ever be topped, since we will likely never come close to playing 45 games again. I cannot explain how we managed that, despite the fact I was the one who scheduled the games.

Matt White has won two games, Kevin Driscoll one, and Mario Ellis two. Our Phenom, and I understand convicts and guards alike are calling Lamarr by that title, has fallen off sharply in his production.

The home run record was set by Eugene Carlisle (also see photo in chapter 1) about twelve years ago—thirteen homers—and he did it in only eight games, surpassing the record of Frank O'Connell's eight. What a player Eugene was, and what a sad story, too. He could have been a big-time ball player, but the gang-related drug wars in nearby Richmond took two members of this family, and Eugene was never able to get the hate out of him.

Following his release from prison, I was contacted by Eugene's sister and later his father. The family wanted to get Eugene involved in something wholesome, so I asked him later on if he wanted to play on the men's baseball league team that Jimbo Guardino had begun. This team was named The Sunset Nine. I had a uniform Jimbo got for me, and it had my last name on the back of it. We played our games at "Big Rec" in the City.

Jimbo was the Pirates catcher during the early years of the Pirates formation. Jimbo and I kept in touch, and he

Eugene Carlisle

asked me one day if I wanted to play on his team. I was over the hill, but I said yes, and I called Eugene and asked him if he wanted to play. He did, and his sister and father brought him to games.

I can still see in my mind's eye the game when I was playing first base (it was hard for Jimbo to hit me), a runner was on first, and Eugene was pitching. This guy could play anywhere, anytime, and excel beyond belief. Anyway, Eugene turned to first out of the stretch and fired a ball, hoping to get the runner out. I had no chance. It was by me in an instant and there I was racing, ha, ha, to get the ball. Oh well, we all had a good laugh about it later on.

I made the mistake of mentioning the home run record to our Phenom a few weeks ago after he hit his third one. He immediately let me know that now he had too much pressure on him. His response was somewhat shocking to me. It was merely a fun kind of remark on my part and not a challenge, but I miscalculated. Since then, no homers from Lamarr; he is flailing away at the plate and mopes around seeking guidance from almost everyone on how to correct his swing.

Dave, our team chaplain, such a fine man, is nearing the end of his playing days. In a critical situation toward the end of the game he was due up. From the on-deck circle he glanced at me standing at the third base coaching box. Did I want him to hit or maybe go with a pinch hitter, is what I surmised was on his mind. He had to hit, though, as no one else was left; he weakly grounded out to the pitcher for the last out with the bases loaded and us down one run. Oh well. Then I saw it in his eyes and heard him comment to another player that maybe he shouldn't be hitting any more.

Dave can still pitch, and he can bunt; his days are not over yet, but that is coming. Next year I will bring Dave back on the team as a coach as well as the chaplain.

My own ball playing days are long gone, but I love the game and am so pleased to be a part of it. Someone asks, "When do we have to give up playing the game?" The answer is, "When they no longer let you take your wheelchair out on the field!" This is how it is for many of us—the game just means that much to us. Maybe a bit unbalanced, for sure, but it gets in your head and heart. Such a difficult game to play with so much opportunity to do poorly, but we keep coming back. I hope Dave will be like that.

Dishon, the guy who talked his way on the team, is still plugging away, but I can tell he is having to deal with the frustration of not being able to crack the starting lineup. He is pressing too hard and not getting the job done. Recently, he was on second base, having walked, and after taking second on a wild pitch, he charged into third base with a big slide on a passed ball and was nearly called out. Trouble is, I had not given him the steal sign. After he dusted himself off, I asked him how come. He told me he wanted to do something for the team. What can you say? (See his photo in chapter 19.)

About the No Name team—I wish they would name themselves, but they probably won't, Anyway, things are okay now. I reserve the right to change my mind. It is too long a story to relate how I came to this, and I am not sure myself. There were apologies, promises, and gestures of good will such as helping out with field maintenance. A couple of the players I respect, such as Paul Jordan and Ke Lamm, talked with me to sort of work things out. At this point in the story, I have scheduled three outside teams to come in and play them.

The umpires are still doing their boycott, but one umpire, Nick Bauer, has broken ranks and is calling the game behind the plate and doing well. A couple of other guys from the No Name team are volunteering to help out on the bases. Looks like another situation solved. There is yet a lot of baseball to be played, and there will be more interesting things coming up.

Left:

Dave Baker, Chaplain of the Team

26
Bad or Good?

Are you as bad as you play? or, Are you as good as you play? Bad and good—I am talking about character or value as a person.

During the preseason phase of the baseball program there is usually a session on how it is that players of any sport think of themselves in terms of their skill level. So often players equate being a good player with being a good person—and in prison this is a serious issue.

Baseball in particular is a game where there is ample opportunity for failure. It is often said that it is a humbling game—one day a hero, the next a goat. Hitting 300 equates to being a great hitter, but it means that you failed seven out of ten times. Recently, a local major league pitcher threw a perfect game then proceeded to lose his next three starts, and none of them were pretty.

It matters little if it is high school baseball or prison ball—players will evaluate themselves on how well they play the game measured by the number of innings and at bats they get—and by, of course, their numbers.

It takes a level of maturity that few reach in prison, I have noticed, to separate performance from personal worth. The heroes are cheered, while the bench players get little or no encouragement. Part of my job as coach is to see that everyone gets into a game from time to time. Today's game against the Willing was one of those times where all except one player got playing time.

The score ended up being a Giants win, 11 to 6, not that close. Matt White pitched five innings, Kevin Driscoll three, and Chris Rich went one. (We only played eight innings due to the extreme length of the game itself, alarms, walks, plus an injured fan who required an ambulance to come get him.)

I wanted Chris to pitch maybe one last inning. He had received word that he might be transferred to a prison in Tracy, California at any time. Chris is the heart and soul of the team and always has been since transferring in from Corcoran Prison down south just to be able to play baseball. The score was 11 to 4 when he entered the game, but he gave up a two-run homer—a mighty blast it was—but at least he got in a game.

Players, no matter what I say, will evaluate themselves according to their baseball success or lack thereof. I can only bring the subject up and hope someone gets it. The guys mostly feel bad enough about themselves without heaping on top of it that they are bad because they don't play baseball as well as others.

I comfort myself by thinking that the players have a chance to work through emotional stuff while on the team. Baseball is a competitive sport, like they all are, and while it is a team sport, it is also an individual one.

It is a game played with emotion, hopefully, and thus a person can have the chance, in a fairly safe way, to come to grips with feelings that may have contributed to their coming to prison in the first place. The lifers, usually those with Murder-2 convictions, if they have been in prison ten or more years and are in a level 2 prison like San Quentin, will often have reached a maturity that has surprised me.

The No Name team played the Giants recently. I was not there, but one of the players on the No Name team went off like a rocket. He was one of those our coaches did not want on the Giants because of exactly what happened at the game in question. At the next game, I received two reports of the situation, one from Chris and the other from an officer in a gun tower who witnessed the whole thing. The officer was disturbed by it and cautioned me about the player who acted wildly. My decision was to remove him from the No Name team in order to prevent another incident that could jeopardize the program.

When I could, I talked to the guy who ran the No Name teams and told him the one player would have to be expelled from the team. It was not well received, but I had to do what I had to do.

What followed was one player after another approaching me and pleading that I would change my mind. I was told they would work with him and help him from going off again. It seemed to me that I was hearing genuine concern and caring. In my heart I wanted to relent, but I knew I could not. For one thing, if the player were allowed to be on the team, I would have to be at every game he played in to be sure there were no problems. This I could not do. Also, I had been put on notice from a correctional officer and guessed he had written up a report on the incident. Any further trouble might end the baseball program—not probable, but possible.

It was due to this situation that I began to think about the subject of this chapter. Here was a player that might have been harmed, to some unknown degree, because of my action. I will worry about it for some time, I suppose, but I will stand by my decision, hoping that a greater good was achieved. Who knows?

In the background, Scott Ostler, my favorite sportswriter of all time, is aiming his camera at the plate. (See also chapter 18 for a photo of him interviewing Chris Rich.)

27
Considering Stretch

He did not presume upon others. He understood limitations. He told me he survived in prison by not entertaining any expectations. As a convict he did not think he had anything coming to him. He had killed his wife with a baseball bat, and he knew he deserved what he got.

"Stretch" is a nick name, because Chris Rich is six feet and nine inches tall. He did not spend his youth in lock ups of one kind or another. He attended St. John's University and pitched the school to national championships his freshman and senior years. A pitching coach with the big-league team that drafted him changed his pitching delivery and ruined Chris's arm, which cost him a bright career in professional baseball. His hopes shattered, he began drinking, and as happens to many who give up inside, he lost himself.

While incarcerated at Corcoran State Prison in California he heard about the baseball program at San Quentin and somehow got himself transferred to SQ so he could play on the team. That may sound strange, but if you knew Chris you would understand. A murderer, alcoholic, convict—yet prison officials, as well as fellow convicts, trust and respect him. So, he came to San Quentin and became the winningest pitcher in the history of baseball at the prison. In 2009, for example, he won the last three games of the season pitching the full twenty-seven innings—all shut outs. In 2010 he has pitched only one inning due to knee surgery at the beginning of the season. He gave up a two-run home run, and I blame myself for rushing him. He is likely done for the year.

Chris has handled all the paperwork for the team—the memos, statistics, and all else that needed to be done inside the walls of the prison, things that I could not do. There is talk that he will be transferred to the Duelle Institute at Tracey, California, and that he will be given an office and will carry the key to it in his pocket. What a loss that will be for us at SQ but a gain for that prison.

Over my now twenty-nine years at San Quentin, I have found few convicts who have not been thoroughly institutionalized.[1] Chris is one of these few. Of course, he had entered prison as an adult, came from a middle class family, and had been educated at a highly respected school. He had no sense of entitlement, no welfare mentality, and no expectations. This season, despite being unable to run, hit, or pitch, he has been pleased to be part of the team doing whatever he could to help.

Earlier this week, on June 21, I had a talk with Chris, and he told me about the possible transfer. He is hoping to stay at San Quentin so he can be with the team till the end of the season.

In his early fifties, Chris has been in prison about fifteen years now and will probably have to do another ten before he is paroled—that is, if the political climate in California remains as it is today.

Chris Rich – "Stretch" (6'9" tall)

---

1   By "institutionalized" I mean a mentality characterized by a sense of "we versus they," a tribal mentality learned when people are locked up from an early age. These unfortunate young people have been cared for, however badly, for much of their lives and expect those in power to take care of them. The enemy for the institutionalized is anyone in authority, and often a baseball coach is part of the "they." It is fairly easy for me to detect the attitudes of entitlement because of my high school baseball coaching experience. I could have used the term "welfare mentality" to describe what I mean, whereby a person expects to be taken care of, managed, and regulated. Such convicts will commonly make demands that are beyond reason. It is part of what it means that a player is a "poison" or a "cancer."

Left from front:

Charles Lyons, Dave Baker, Chris Rich, Kevin Loughlin

28
Santa Monica Suns

On June 26, Saturday, the Santa Monica Suns played the Giants a double-header. I look forward to this team coming in more than any other. After the first game, which ends about 12:30 p.m., we head for the Marin Brewery in Larkspur for lunch, after which the team comes back to the prison for the second game. Not sure how the team contacted me, but Bob Sharka and Peter Cook have been bringing in the team now for three years.

H Unit, wherein Matt, Henry, Mario, Rico, and Dishon are housed, was quarantined due to the outbreak of a virus, which meant three pitchers gone, along with our short stop and our best bats. The Suns are not a bunch of kids, but they play a lot of ball and know the game. In game one, Peter Cook pitched seven innings and did very well. Kevin Driscoll started for the Giants and had a tough outing. Marcus Crum had to catch; there was absolutely no one else, since Johnnie was helping on a charity food sale. When Johnnie told me about his commitment, I did my best to talk him out of it. No, it was going to be Marcus behind the plate.

Marcus—ghetto black, young, not good looking, barely educated, and with a very long sentence—he has tried hard but simply cannot play the game very well. He has gotten so little playing time that I was sure he would quit the team, but he did not; he hung in there, despite spending most of his time on the bench. Now was his chance, and he did poorly behind the plate nearly the whole game.

The Suns jumped out to a two-run lead in the first, and we didn't score until the fourth—two runs that tied the game. Then in the fifth, the Suns scored three runs, and we were three behind. At the end of the top of the fifth, Kevin came out and threw his glove against the screen and shouted out a stream of ugly complaints about Marcus who was dropping about 40% of the pitches Kevin was throwing. I was already in the third base coach's box and had to be summoned to calm things down.

After order was restored and I was back in the box, another loud argument broke out, this time involving the issue of throwing equipment. One guy, a veteran, took it upon himself to educate Kevin about the unwritten rule, and that turned out to be a mistake. Back I went again, and I had to quickly explain that I did not get too twitterpated (one of my favorite words) about the emotional side of the game. I glanced at Marcus and saw that the pain of his ordeal was evident on his face, yet he had no choice than to stay and play.

Kevin was done, and there was only one other pitcher available—Dave Baker, our team chaplain. Dave's playing days were almost over. He knew it, but he still loved the game and was always hoping to get another outing. But if Dave pitched in the first game there would be no one to pitch the evening game. My problem was obvious, and Chris Rich approached me and said he could do it. His knee surgery apparently was not a bother any longer, but the layoff meant he was out of shape. But he did come in, Kevin moved to third base, Stafont grabbed some pine, and we went to the bottom of the fifth.

It was one of the moments I wait for. A couple of men on base with no outs and I could set the wheels in motion. By the time we had two outs we had two runs and needed only one more to tie up the game. The Phenom, Lamarr King, got a walk, stole second, and advanced to third on a passed ball. (The Phenom's play, especially his hitting, has dropped off so dramatically that Phenom is no longer a name he wants to hear.)

Now James Bautista was up, without question our best bunter and fastest man to first base on the team. While the Suns battery was composing itself after the passed ball, James came up the line, and we decided to do a suicide squeeze on the second pitch. Even with two outs there was a good chance of scoring the run. James laid a perfect bunt down the first base line, and though Peter Cook, the pitcher, got to it quickly, James slid head first into the base ahead of the throw, and we scored the run, but at a price—James severely damaged his knee.

Then I had to leave the game to perform a wedding at the Inn Marin in Novato. Kevin Loughlin took over and managed the rest of the game. I left the yard with my son, Vernon, as Chris was warming up getting ready to pitch the sixth. (Vern is taking over coaching the prison's 8-man flag football team I started six years ago and no longer have the time and energy to do.)

Weddings—I have done almost 1,500 of them over the years—a way I have of making extra money. Baptist preachers don't usually make much money, so a wedding is a big deal to me. And due to the baseball on Saturdays, it is rare I get to take a wedding, but I did not realize it would mean missing the usual lunch at the Marin Brewery in Larkspur. The hamburgers, the beer, and mostly the conversation was something I looked forward to. It was three o'clock when I finally made it, time for only an iced tea, but spending time with the guys was special.

At four thirty I was back at the East Gate for the second game. It took awhile to get the convicts out of North Block and down on the field. It seemed an eternity before we were ready to play the game. As yet, I did not know how the morning game had turned out, but in a short while I learned that Chris had pitched the entire rest of the game and gave up only one run–I was shocked!

So it was that in the bottom of the ninth the score was 6 to 5 in favor of the Suns. Marcus came up and had not done a thing in his previous at bats, but now he smacked a solid double, and Elliot was able to get him home, tying the game. That was how it ended, since time had run out. A tie—our first such of the year. Wow, I felt happy for Marcus—just what he needed.

Marcus Crumm

Then the evening game. Dave Baker pitched and got the only hit while giving up twelve runs. It would have been a lot worse except for a couple of brilliant defensive plays by the Giants.

I don't recall making one call all game. Throughout the entire game, the team was quiet and subdued. Marcus did not play in the game at all, since Johnnie was available for the second game, but he sat right next to me the whole time I was in the dugout. We talked about everything—his growing up, his crime, his future or what there might be of it, and I found him to be a witty, bright, and interesting young man.

He told me about growing up in Oakland, not exactly sure who his father was. He hit the streets early and had joined a notorious street gang. He made some good money and for a short time lived the fast, crazy life with cool clothes and a fast car. As we sat on the bench, I never felt a single twinge of fear or disgust for someone who had probably hurt some folks. At times we laughed together, sometimes shared sadness that was in Marcus' life. Here was a rather pleasant and smart young man who was part of a particularly murderous gang.

After the second game, Bob Sharka asked me if I could let the guys see some of the prison, and I thought that if I took them up the long staircase leading to North Block on the way out instead of up Cardiac Hill that runs on the north side of the new hospital, they could see a little of the prison. Fourteen of us, twelve Suns with Mike Deeble and me, trudged up the steps only to be greeted by a lieutenant who informed me I was not to do what I was doing. He sounded stern, even like my error would cost me in some way, but he suddenly lightened up and started to engage the players. It turned out to be an okay time.

Johnny Taylor

A play at the plate and Johnny is ready.

As we left the Mac Shack and the lieutenant, I stopped a little way down in front of an incredible wall mural depicting themes popular with convicts. I pointed out where the old condemned row was, where their yard was, and why new men with a capital sentence are housed initially, and sometimes for years, in the Adjustment Center, a prison within a prison, learning to adjust to the fact they would not leave the prison alive and could be executed at any time.

As Johnny makes the play, at the fence, from left to right: wife Katie, Jim Parker, and Scott Ostler

There was a pronounced surreal feel, as we talked together, the guys in their bright white uniforms and thir equipment bags, in a fairly tight circle listening to an old coach talk about some of the things he knew about prison life.

One point in that conversation stands out as I type this just now. One of the guys asked what would happen to him if he came to prison. My answer was that without a gang, or a car,[1] he would be taken advantage of, unless he

---

1   "Car" means an inmate group you are considered to be part of, thus having some protection. A gang is a car; the baseball team would be a car—any group in fact—and without one, well, not good. Few can cope alone.

was able to stand up and fight back. Being taken advantage of might mean having to buy things for some bully at the cantine with your own money, or giving your dessert to someone else, or performing a sex act or allowing one to be performed on you. This is certainly a short list.

The sad reality is that a man comes into prison either as predator or prey. And it may be more dangerous to be a predator—one never relaxes. Being in prison means being stressed all the time. One ages much more quickly in prison than out. Of course, this is not entirely true, especially in a prison like San Quentin, but it is true for many.

Right: Kent and Marcus doing "in and out" prior to the game.

Below: Scorekeepers also help the game proceed.

29

The Field

Earlier I mentioned that the grass for "The Field of Dreams" was given to the prison by the San Francisco Giants Baseball Club. Over the years we have attempted to keep it up. One year I bought sprinkler heads, since a number were broken and had to be replaced. This took two years and was never done properly. After weeks of fooling with the system, two heads were left off and when the timer signaled for the watering to start, the outcome was two little lakes formed, both in right field.

For the last two years we have wanted to reseed the outfield, bring in more infield dirt, and generally refurbish the field at no cost to the state. Prison officials are still talking about how to get it done.

Over the years there have been many issues. We are now out of means to line or stripe the infield—those white lines that help us tell when a ball is fair or foul, and other things, too. There are three hefty bags of lye at the prison, in industry[1], but it is virtually impossible for us to get hold of them, though they are there with the intent of being used by the team.

This may sound like a whine, or something like that, but here is a fictitious account of what often goes on. (Actually, this is quite close to being a true story.):

Let us say that a light bulb needs replacing—it burned out. A request is made by a staff person for a new light bulb, by phone. That was not good enough; the request had to be written in the form of a memo. (A memo is like a commandment of God written in stone.) The memo was written. It went to maintenance and was lost for about one year. A new memo was written up. It made its way to maintenance, and a requisition form was made out for a new light bulb. In the meantime, the head of maintenance retired, and several

---

1   *Industry* is what is behind the massive wall running along the right field line, from the top of Cardiac Hill to H Unit. Behind the wall is where the convicts make all sorts of stuff, and it is considered a desirable job and even earns the guys some money, which is credited to them at the canteen.

other maintenance staff took over, until Sacramento appointed a new head of maintenance. When the position was filled, it was necessary for a new memo to be written. A request was made for a new bulb. Months went by. Finally, the person who needed the light bulb, the bulb that lighted the windowless room where the sports equipment was stored, asked for an electrician to come down and fix the problem. A memo was made out for this, and sometime later, an electrician showed up but did not have the right equipment. Eventually, the right stuff was located, and a new light fixture, not just a new bulb, was installed. I was informed right away, because a whole lot of baseball equipment was stored in the dark room, and we needed it badly. So, the great day came, and we went down to the room, unlocked the door, flipped the light switch and it didn't work. Dark. The room is still dark.

Back to the field. It is July 13 as I am writing this. I received a call from the prison informing me the grass in the outfield was dead, except for some in right field. I guess I was expected to do something about it.

What was I going to do about it? I explained we could water it by hand as we do when we wet down the infield before a ball game. No, that was out of the question. No reason was given when I asked "Why?" Okay, I said, I guess you will have to figure a way. Well, my caller said, looks like your field of dreams is history.[2]

Left:

The most green to be seen!

---

2   I am editing this chapter on December 30, 2010. Last week we were finally given the go ahead to work on the field. Kevin Loughlin had everything lined up, and it would cost him personally a lot of money. But it rained too heavily the day before the workday, so everything had to be called off. We will try again this coming Saturday.

We can see right field in these photos. Top photo Kevin Driscoll is hitting, bottom photo is Redd Casey.

30
Goodbye Chris

More now on Stretch, 6'9", but I call him Chris. Rarely would I use jail house nicknames, but Stretch was so named for his stature. Tall and skinny, college education, fifteen years down and not eligible to go to the board until late 2016, for second degree murder—he killed his wife with a baseball bat.

Last night, July 14, Chris pitched his last game at San Quentin. Today he is being transferred to Tracy, to the Duelle Institute, where he will have his own office with a key to the door. Such is the respect the man has earned in the California State prison system.

The opposing team was none other than Elliot Smith's Oaks/Cubs, a team that has been coming in for fifteen years, so everyone on the team knew Chris well. I had intended to start Chris, but he said he would rather watch than play—unusual for him.

Henry started, a rough first inning, but he gave up only one run, and that run unearned. H Unit had been shut down for two weeks, meaning that Henry and the rest of the guys there could not work out with the team. I asked Henry—his full name is Kevin Henry, but he goes by Henry—if he was ready and he said yes. He pitched three full innings, but with one out in the fourth he was done. Suspecting as much, I had earlier approached Chris and asked him to get ready. The other team had firmly pressed me to pitch Chris, since they knew it would be their last chance to face him. Chris hesitated for a moment then went down to the bull pen to loosen up.

When I knew Chris was ready, I walked out and got the ball from Henry but put him in left field in place of Duck, because I needed Henry's bat. I waited for Chris to come all the way to the mound, and I stuck the baseball in his glove and said, "This is the last time I will hand you the ball, Chris."

On Chris's second pitch he got a double play grounder to short and we were still up by one run, 3 to 2. He sailed through the fifth, but after two outs in the sixth, which would be our last inning, he gave up four runs. No way was I going to remove him, so I had no one warming up. His last inning would be the way it would be.

Last of the sixth, score 6 to 3, it looked like we were cooked. Lamarr, the phenom, led off and struck out in an ugly way. His phenom status had not lasted long, and it might be that I must DH for him soon. Awful is the only way to describe his hitting now. Oh, by the way, Dishon has disappeared—not enough playing time I assume, and Dave Baker, team chaplain, had shoulder surgery and is out for the season. We have gone from twenty-two to seventeen players now, and Chris's loss will reduce us to sixteen, the exact number I said we would be left with.

Mario, an H Unit guy, looking rusty at bat and on the field, nevertheless hit a towering home run over the left field fence. We were all amazed. 6 to 4 now. But one out and no one on.

A hit and an error later we had runners on first and second. The next hitter got the bunt sign; now there were two outs with runners on second and third. Red Casey, number four hitter who had driven in runs number two and three, was up next, but he received an intentional pass. Chris Marshall was up next, and he muscled one out between left and center. The score was tied. Bilal, whom I call the Rock, had "dropped a can of corn" (fumbled an easy pop-up catch) in the first inning which had resulted in a run; he was now up. I walked down the line and told Bilal the suicide squeeze was on, first pitch. Mike Tyler, pinch runner at third, got the same message.

Bilal Chatman

It would have to be a perfect bunt. Mike charged in with the pitch, Bilal squared and laid down a little roller that got by the pitcher and was too far from the first baseman for him to make a play; they just watched the ball roll.

Mike hit the plate; Bilal hit the bag, game over. The Oaks/Cubs were in shock. The Giants went wild, jumping around and hooting, and we lined up as usual for the high fives with the opposing team.

For me, though, it meant the loss of Chris Rich. A little group of cons and Oaks/Cubs players gathered around him to say goodbye. I went to the dugout and got my equipment bag ready to go. Chris has been one of the chief reasons I had stayed with the baseball program. He made things easy, did all the paperwork, which there was a bunch of, and simply handled things for me and the rest of the team. Things will now be different, and I don't know how right now.

As I was heading up Cardiac Hill, I turned to see Chris watching me leave as he stood with a little group on the mound, a little space in San Quentin that he loved. I raised my hand to him, he did the same, and some tears came to my eyes, just as they are right now as I write this.

Chris "Stretch" Rich

31
Disappointments

Dishon talked his way onto the team. For two weeks or more I told him it was too late, but he persisted. I relented, brought him on the team, got him a pair of spikes, and let him use my good outfielders 12-inch, heart-of-the-hide glove. A mistake?

He was not patient, not a team player. He certainly had skills—speed, arm, hitting; but he didn't really know the game. Probably his only baseball experience had been little league, where he would have been an all star. When he didn't get enough playing time with the Giants he started whining, showing up late for games, and just generally dogging it.

A few times I tried to communicate with him. It seemed that I encountered anger in him, which in a place like SQ would be no surprise. He was distant now and did not want to sit and talk about the game. Perhaps I had merely been conned—he had gotten what he wanted and had now lost interest. Who knows?

Giants players made a point of telingl me that I should cut him officially from the team instead of simply waiting to see if he would show up. I understood, but I held on, just in case. Maybe there was a chance to help the young man, turn him around so that he would not spend most of his life behind bars. Yes, I have some of the "do gooder" mentality in me.

After a month and a half with no Dishon, it was time to announce he was no longer a Giant, which I did and that was it. Walking out of the prison that evening I felt the disappointment, the sadness, and determined once again that such discouragements must not make me callous. There would be more Dishons.

Then the Phenom. Another disappointment. His performance has continued to slide, and the whining and complaining has continued. He shows up for the games on time but goes off by himself and takes forever to get his gear and uniform on. The last several games he has taken so much time getting ready that he has missed warmups—the running, throwing, and stretching—yet he still expects to find his name on the lineup card. When I explain to him that he is not ready to go and that he must find a way to get his warmup work in, he snarls at me and insists he is ready to go. No, I will not give in, and when I tell him so, he turns his back on me and walks away.

This coming week I intend to have a talk with him and explain that he is spinning himself off the team. A couple of our coaches talked the situation over recently, and we all agreed he was becoming a cancer on the bench. Maybe he needs to find out the hard way that his way of doing business is not working. Very likely his ways have not ever worked and may have been a contributing factor to his being in prison.

People like me who volunteer at prisons think we may be able to make a difference in someone's life. We see few successes, however, and are tempted to give up and turn cynical. It is easy to think the cons are incorrigible and beyond hope—many come to that. From time to time, I remind myself that all I see is a snapshot in time and not the end of the story. A troubling event is not all there is.

There was a hard core con nicknamed Animal some years back—a fighter, lots of fist fights, and he thought he was a great catcher—he wasn't. Down more than twenty years already, he thought he would die in prison. My experience with him made me think he might be right.

If anyone tried out for catcher, Animal was against him. One year he lost his starting position, and I thought he would act out and put the baseball program in jeopardy. I had to confront him one practice, and I was afraid of the outcome. After listening awhile to what I had to say I could almost see the smoke coming out of his ears. That was the end of it for him; he quit the team.

Amazingly he began to change. Mr. Bad Man started going to the chapel, and slowly, little by little, he was becoming someone much more content with himself and his lot. The fierce anger that was usually evident on his face was gone. When he caught up with me on the yard one day, we had a pleasant conversation. One of the last times we talked together, he told me he had been given a date by the parole board, first time ever. Usually, he would be denied two or more years.

Animal did not die in prison; he has been home now for several years, and I hear that he is doing well. Could it be that his experience with the baseball program made a difference in his life? I will probably never know.

32
16 Wins, 10 Losses, 1 Tie

Our record was 35 wins and 10 losses in 2008, then 6 wins and 15 losses in 2009. With one month left in our 2010 season, during which we may play as many as nine games, it is still possible to have a losing season. It has happened before, of course—twice in my time at the prison—but as I survey the schedule, I figure we should be all right.

In years past the Giants twice lost four games in a row. At San Quentin that is a serious losing streak, and the blaming can take an ugly turn. Two weeks ago, we were at 15 wins, 7 losses, and one tie. (The tie—the Santa Monica Suns won the morning game, and the evening game was tied when we had to end the game for the Close B custody guys to get counted on time.) But we had three losses in a row—all while Katie and I were away visiting her dad in West Virginia. The Rebel Giants beat us, as did the Willing,[1] and then the Longhorns got us in a close game. The Longhorns, managed by Lenny Vagt, always beats us. This team is actually the baseball team at the College of San Mateo in the South Bay.

What a sight it is to see this team come down Cardiac Hill as they make their way to the Lower Yard and the Field of Dreams. Young baseball players, and a whole bunch of them, in the sharpest looking uniforms you can imagine—quite a sight, and the Giants as well as the whole yard stop everything to watch the procession. Wish I could have been there to see it this year.

Another reason I hated to miss the Longhorns game was because Lenny had Ed Montague with him, one of the revered major league umpires from the old days. And what a gentleman I heard he was! He graciously signed the bill of each of our player's caps. Several players told me it was a

---

[1] The Willing, not a good name for outsiders in a prison—you can guess why—but made up of guys I knew outside, high school kids I coached and some of their fathers. We wore the Washington Nationals baseball caps, with the W. This footnote is added in 2020, and I am still doing the same.

day they will never forget. Other players were wondering how much the caps might sell for on eBay.

I got back from West Virginia to manage the game, July 31, against The Mission. This team, led by Greg Snyder, from San Francisco's Mission District, is one of my favorites. Guys mostly in their thirties who play a good game, but we usually beat them. And we did it again behind Henry's pitching with Rico coming in for the save. It was a bigger deal than it might seem, since the whites in North Block were locked down.

Locked down means the prisoners affected are not allowed out of their cells, except to shower once or twice a week. Meals are taken to them in their cells, but no yard, no exercise, nothing. A white convict in North Block had been murdered by another white. It was not racially motivated. Vengeance by proxy, maybe, but there would be repercussions, although the murderer had been caught instantly. Maintaining control of the prison often means doing something that has a far-reaching impact. If a whole class of people is penalized, the reasoning goes, the convicts will police themselves. And it mostly works, since so much is lost in a wholesale lock down—school classes, chapel, visits, and sports on the lower yard—all cancelled. Locking down the whites was a reasonable response.

It has happened that a game could not be played due to a lock down, especially when the whites and blacks are locked down at the same time. If the whole of North Block is locked down, there would be no game at all. After the tryouts in late February, early March, and we have a good idea of who will make the team, the housing of the players is examined. It is best to have as even a balance of players on the team as possible in terms of race.

During the month of June, there tend to be more lock downs than during any other time of the year. The reason for this is in the California State budget. Fewer officers are needed with a lock down going on, thus a savings. This year we saw the lower yard closed the last two weeks of June, and we were told it had to do with staffing issues—which, when translated, means budget trouble.

San Quentin is a prison, and security is foremost. I never complain or take cancellation issues personally. It is a privilege to even be there. Some volunteers lose sight of this fact and act as though they have a right to do as they please—after all, they are giving up their precious time. This attitude is one I correct, and quickly, if I hear it from someone I am responsible for. More than one volunteer in the baseball program has been told they are no longer needed if they keep failing to understand they are involved with convicted felons, many of whom are murderers, rapists, and other scary things. Solid volunteers who are a credit to the institution are few and far between.

Left: Kevin Henry—big man and knew how to play the game.

Below: Kevin hits one over the right field fence.

33
Fear Is the Reason

August 4, Wednesday, 4:50 p.m., shortly after count had cleared and after checking in at 4 Post and the MAC Shack, I walked down the long flight of stairs to the east side of the lower yard, which was entirely devoid of any signs of life. It would be a while before an officer was found to work the yard, and I figured I would be able to stretch out on the Giants bench and close my eyes for a few minutes.

Somehow Chris Marshall appeared, then Orlando "Duck" Harris, seemingly from nowhere. When I asked how they got there, they told me they were working in the education building and would have gone back to North Block but instead just decided to head for the ball field. I knew that was against the rules, since there was no cop on the lower yard, but I let it go. It was not likely I would lose my volunteer card if someone were to raise the issue.

Often in previous years I took the team to the outfield grass, where we would sit down and talk. I had loved those times, but it had been years since something like that happened. Now I thought being alone with Chris and Duck,[1] both black men and three strikers, would give me a chance to get to know them better.

Before I could get started, Chris told me that he, Johnnie, and Bilal had met with the Phenom and had talked some sense into him. Chris promised that Lamarr would no longer be a problem. (As it turned out, he was right.)

Now that business was taken care of, we began to talk, just the three of us. Orlando started off with the usual convict idea that the correctional system in California was a business and a cash cow at that. He mentioned the long sentences given to three strikers,[2] and how it costs the state $50,000 a

---

1   At the time of this footnote, January of 2020, Duck is still at SQ, and we see each other occasionally. He has helped the baseball program so very much, and we will always be friends. Can hardly wait for him to get out.

2   The Three Strikes law aimed at repeat offenders—three strikes or three fel-

year to incarcerate each convict. Chris was agreeing with every statement.

Orlando spoke his piece and paused, giving me a chance to respond. I opened with what I had seen in the late 1960s and early 1970s when I first started coming to the prison. Then there were few blacks and Hispanics; most of the prisoners were white and older than the population now at the prison. Many were career criminals who talked about their style of crime as though they were ordinary businessmen. Then, around the early 1970s a change, a radical change, took place. I saw San Quentin fill up with young offenders, most of them black, some Hispanics, and lots of young whites. The major reason for the influx was dope, and everybody knew it.

Right: Chris Marshall, solid player; saw him last at the prson in 2020, and he told me he was on his way home.

Drugs, sex, and rock and roll—the big three, and the prison population mushroomed, requiring ever more prisons to be built. Dope does produce some disastrous results, and it became clear that a civilized people could simply not tolerate the raping, robbing, and murdering that came with the liberating times.

Everyone saw the evening television broadcasts—raping, robbing, and murdering—and it made people afraid. Yes, fear was behind the growth in the prison population. If a person was going to do bad things, they had to be removed from society. Plain and simple. I even agreed that the business paradigm might have some credit to it, but that was secondary.

Chris and Duck did not say much in response, but it seemed my argument made sense to them. Perhaps they were thinking back to the crimes that led to their three strike sentences. After all, and everybody knows it, you don't get to San Quentin by being a model citizen; in fact, it is not easy to wind up in the prison. No, you have to work at it.

---

ony convictions and you are put away for a very long time—served to fatten up the number of convicts in the state prisons, which many convicts say is good for business. The $50,000 a year is at least doubled at this date, 2020.

Left:

Orlando Harris, known in the yard as Duck, worked in the Sports Director's office and helped us a great deal. Well respected by all.

Below:

Duck making a throw from right field.

34

Frustration

The Fog, a team from San Francisco, of course, came into the prison with five guys on Saturday, August 7. They needed a catcher, an infielder, an outfielder, and a pitcher. No sense in getting upset with the guys who were there, but a bunch of guys who had been cleared in failed to show up. At least it gave some Giants who ordinarily did not get much playing time a chance to play, even if it was for the opposing team. Once all the guys showed up at the field and after noting the lack of players, I decided that Marcus would catch, Stafont would play third, Terry would be the outfielder, and Rico would pitch. I threw Mike in as well, just to get him some playing time. The Fog batted ten and rotated one position player. I was left with eleven players, and I would bat everyone—every Giant would get to play some ball.

Mario pitched, and behind him there was only Henry, and we needed him in left field. How we miss Matt White, the guy who started our opening day game and quickly proved to be the team's best hitter. He went to court to deal with some minor charges nearly two months ago, and we will probably never see him again. I was told he wanted to clear any issues up, so that when he was released he wouldn't have to face any other legal problems.

As I stood in the third base coach's box at the bottom of the first inning, I saw that more than half of The Fog were our players. Oh well, I had to repress my frustration.

Right away we were behind two runs. The Giants were using their softball swings, looping upward through the strike zone and not coming close to doing the job. Signs were missed and base running was bad, but mainly it was a failing to do the most simple and fundamental parts of baseball—catching and throwing the ball.

Take a ground ball or a fly ball. Three things must happen. The ball must be caught, the player must set before throwing the ball, and then there is the throw. Each is separate and distinct act.

The catch—seeing the ball into the glove—is where the play starts, even though there is a step or two prior to the catch: positioning and thinking through what to do with the ball should it be hit to you. Yes, baseball is more mental than physical, contrary to popular understanding. It is not too rare to see a major league ball player, making a few million dollars, take his eye off the ball just before the catch is made; bad things can follow. At the crucial moment in the game, in the last inning with the score tied, Johnnie looked up to see where a runner charging in from third was and missed a perfect throw to the plate. (See a photo of Johnnie in chapter 5.) Then he picked up the ball and without setting his feet fired the ball into left field trying to get a runner coming into third. Two runs scored, and we lost the game by those two runs.

Left: Stafont Smith—enjoyed the game and played hard.

Mr. Double may become Johnnie's nick name—double after double, three doubles in yesterday's game—and without them the Giants would have had almost no offense.

Johnnie is our team captain with Chris Rich now gone. And we got word about what happened to Chris, but the info is still in the rumor stage. Apparently, once aboard the bus to take him to the prison in Tracy, he was told there was no room there, so he went to a prison called Avenal instead. May or may not be true, but when I find out I will report it here.

Rico, our own pitcher, and I had not thought a very good one, completely shut us down and got the win, a win for The Fog. He is Puerto Rican and speaks both Spanish and English perfectly. He has earned a start for sure. Then there's Dominique, the young man who got a fifty-year-to-life sentence for a murder he swears he did not commit—fifty years because it was gang related. He got three at-bats and played a very credible right field. It was his throw that Johnnie bungled. I was really surprised. It may be that I consistently undervalued him. To his credit, though I could tell he was discouraged, he did not quit. The best thing about Dominique is his hair dos and how he arranges his dew rags.

After the catch is setting to throw. Johnnie's errors would not have mattered so much had not Redd tossed a ball into left field trying to make an easy double play. He threw off balance despite having plenty of time. See the ball into the glove, the catch, set and make the throw. Three separate and distinct plays. A simple game, really, catching and throwing the ball.

Right: Mike Tyler—good base runner, very fast.

35

Sports in Prison

The subject is boys and men—those members of the human family that have testosterone in them, and some more than others. Females have estrogen, and I think it works differently for the ladies than the male hormone does for men. This is not a biology lecture, but my thesis is that men should be given some legitimate and acceptable way to discharge their testosterone surges.

High school kids playing football get concussions from time to time. Once in a while, a kid gets hit in the head with a thrown or batted ball and 911 is called. Then follows loud pleas to end violent sports for youth up to and including college age young people.[1] But it won't happen. Better equipment will come along; sports will continue.

Sports in prison? Imagine you are still in the flower of your youth, or not, or maybe you are seeing the signs of aging creeping up on you, and all you have is nothing to do. Read, walk, talk, sleep—boredom can drive people crazy and can even inspire acts of deadly violence for no other reason than it is something to do.

Testosterone is a sex hormone, at least partly so, and there is very little normal and natural sex in prison—just hundreds, even thousands of youngish men with nothing to do and no girl friends or wives, just a body that must be repressed. Let me make it clear that most convicts will avoid homosexuality if they can. San Quentin has a group of homosexuals, and queens can be seen on the lower yard, but the gays are pushed to the fringe, and none, due to the convicts own policing, are allowed to play in the major prison sports. Let me make it clear—this is not my doing. Rapists or cons with crimes against children or even women are usually discriminated against.

There is self sex, which turns out to be more frustrating than satisfy-

---

1   For any parent whose child has been impacted or debilitated by a sports related injury, I mean no callous disregard, rather I have some experience with the sadness such a parent is bound to have.

ing. But sports—here is something that may be an asset to men who cannot turn off the secretions from the adrenal and other glands.

Left: James Bautista batting—played second base and often was lead-off hitter.

The lady cop that I mentioned earlier who sometimes works the lower yard creates some sexual tension when she hangs out by the diamond. She is obviously a well-endowed woman, even in her uniform with a flak jacket on. And she is studiously observed by the cons. She is not flirty or flaunty; she is business-like, but she laughs and smiles and is right there, up close. I see guys stand behind her with their hands deep in their pockets; I doubt she knows about it. Not a chance that I would say anything to anybody. It is largely harmless, I suppose, and as it is said, there but for the grace of God go I.

Right: The San Quentin fans along third base line.

Consider the money side of prison sports—the cost effectiveness or tax dollars. It costs the State of California very little to operate a prison recreation program. The baseball, softball, soccer, and football programs cost the state nothing at all. Over the fifteen years I have been doing baseball, and football for six years, the state has not been billed even a penny. The volunteer coaches take care of it. The San Francisco Giants send us leftover gear. We improvise and make it work.

Another thing: Even if a convict is not able to be on a team due to one thing or another, they can be fans and engage in the conversations and trash talk that goes along with the game. Of course, there is the thrill of seeing whether a wager will pay off.

Growing up in north L.A., I noticed that the gang-bangers were not athletes and vice versa. Maybe the jocks got enough on the field or the court; they did not need or have time for being a cool bad dude. Without school sports, might the prison population be much greater than it is? Somebody needs to do a study on this, maybe get a grant from the state to fund it.

Below: One of the Basketball Teams at SQ

36

"I knew the gun was loaded, but I didn't think it'd kill."

Maybe nine seasons ago, I had a conversation with a player who quoted the words I am using for the title of this chapter. He got them from the song "Smuggler's Blues" that was used as background music for the TV series Miami Vice. He told me, "That's what happened to me."

It was toward the end of a dreary season, and we were getting thumped badly by a team we should have beat easily. Keeping a team sharp all season is not automatic. Players have injuries; they can lose focus and stop caring, and when that happens, they start showing frustration and anger. Not a big surprise, of course, but it presents a challenge. If a fight were to break out, or anything close to it, it could mean the end of baseball at the prison. And one thing I do, the bottom line is—safeguard the program.

The Giants are not in any league, thus there are no standings and no playoff games to shoot for. We start in March with practices, games against outside teams begin in April, and by the middle of August, even I can hardly wait for the last game to go into the books.

He knew the gun was loaded, and what a beautiful piece of art it was. He described it as nickel plated, ivory handles, gilded with gold. The nine-millimeter was awarded to, I will call him Jose, by his gang after he successfully proved himself worthy of being a member of the gang.

When I asked how he'd earned the piece he started then decided against answering. He said I would probably think badly about him if I knew.

So he had this gun, which he never did practice with but carried everywhere he went, carried it in his waistband and flashed it if girls were around. He pulled it out once when he was drunk, and an older member snatched it out of his hand before anything could happen—this in a crowded club in the City, when someone made the mistake of bumping him while he was dancing with some young girl.

We sat and talked on the bench. The outs were coming slowly, a wind had come up, and the temperature was dropping. My attention was on the story I was hearing while the game slogged on.

His people had given him a gun, and he knew at some point he would have to use it. If they gave an order, there was no getting out of it. He'd heard stories of guys reneging and being killed as a result. Even if he had to shoot a relative—no excuses accepted.

The money was flowing. Not only were his people bringing in the dope; they were delivering directly to the customer. The profits soured, and he had all the ladies he wanted, his own place, a car, clothes, and all that went with being a feared member of a powerful gang.

Then things went wrong. Some guys were killed by a gang his people had once muscled out of the drug business and were now mounting a comeback. The San Francisco police had brought in the Feds and arrests were being made. This was when the kill order was communicated to him while he was eating a burrito in a joint in the Mission on 24th Street.

I asked him whom he was supposed to kill, but he would not tell me, which was what I expected. Still, he had never fired his weapon. What he did was to watch television shows where people were shooting each other—to get used to the idea. He paused and said he really had no idea that someone would really die, get shot and die, bleed and scream, and be no more forever. It was hard for him to imagine that the heavy piece of shiny metal he played with all the time could hurt somebody.

He knew the gun was loaded, but he didn't think it'd kill. And it was just like that until "everything exploded, and the blood began to spill." Wow, just like in the song.

Right: Going over the signs prior to the start of a game.

Coach hitting infield before the start of a game.

37
Having a Mission

When you are twenty-five years old and have a fifty-years-to-life sentence, you have to figure a way to keep from going crazy. If not, guys have told me, you should just go ahead and kill yourself or get yourself killed.

You can end it all by attacking someone and refusing to stop after the guard in the tower makes his first warning shot. You don't want to commit a murder, because that would send you to condemned row where life is really boring and bad, since no one is being executed these days, and it is not easy to get away with a suicide.

Dope is a way out—yes, you can get almost anything, but at a very high price, which I don't want to explain.

If you act crazy, look and talk depressed, you can get free dope, dispensed by a medical type each and every day. Not only that, you get a cell on the first tier and are released from your cell to go to chow before anyone else. The medical people who visit the blocks from 3 p.m. to 4 p.m. each day make sure you swallow the pills, so not much hope there.

If you want to live, then you have to have a mission, which is not such a different goal from anyone else, locked up or not. But inside there is not a whole big menu to chose from.

Education is one way to go—get a degree, learn something. San Quentin has this going as well or better than any prison in America. Chapel—and there are choices: Protestant, Catholic, Muslim, Jewish, American Indian, and probably others I am not aware of. Sing in a choir, get into the Bible, try to meet one of the ladies who come in with outside church groups, and yes there have been weddings which can lead to a conjugal visit. Sadly, not all these romances made in heaven work out when the prisoner is released.

Some may not believe what I am about to divulge—some of the finest men I have ever known have been convicts incarcerated at San Quentin, and most of these have been murderers. Some of the saddest cases, the fearsomest crazy people I have ever known, have also been convicts at SQ. The difference? A mission.

Outlive your mother—maybe the number one motivator. Stay alive for your kids, or see if you can contact a son or daughter. Try to figure yourself out—education and a serious relationship with your counselor. Become a jail house lawyer and maybe find a way to legally get out of prison. Almost no one thinks they can escape these days; the corrections people have figured all those angles out, because the political fallout for even an attempt is not pleasant. So, forget that route.

Not a few take up music or art. Chris Rich learned to play a pretty good lead guitar, and Popeye played a so-so trumpet and for a decade or more gave us a rendition of the Star-Spangled Banner each opening day. Not a few books have been written, nearly all either political in nature or autobiographical. John Neblett, our faithful equipment guy, has learned to act and loves Shakespeare. (Since some knew that I wrote books and even published some, I have been given a few manuscripts over the years.)

Baseball—another mission. The game has meant a lot to many a convict. It also has been a source of frustration and sadness to others, and there are a few on the team right now who are facing the ending of their playing days.

Left: Dominique Oden—fast and smart

Chaplain Dave will almost certainly be through as a player after this season. I can see it in Dave's face. He had surgery on his left shoulder and apparently, he is worse off now, the pain being worse now than before. He sits and watches in his state blues and is plainly not his old self. He will have to find another mission, but I suspect he already has one. Dave, in my estimation, would be an ideal neighbor to have, someone you could trust and depend on.

Dominique, a guy with an actual fifty-year sentence, is not going to make it as a baseball player. Wish he would, but no, I will not bring him back next year for too many reasons. Dishon, who got on the team late, disappeared and then suddenly reappeared but disappeared again—no he will have to find another mission. The Phenom is way too complicated for me to figure out. He probably will come out for the team next year, and that will present me with a real dilemma.

Right: Dominique interviewed by KQED

Bilal, whom I have come to call "The Rock," is not as good as I thought he was. He has a long sentence and will certainly show up for the tryouts in 2011.[1] Another dilemma. If I didn't know about missions, it would all be easier for me. How long can James Bautista keep it going? Terry, early fifties now, long sentence, loves the game so much and works so hard. He dresses the field, rakes, waters, hustles—probably the smartest ball player on the team. He is nearing the end of his days as a baseball player. Orlando, otherwise known as Duck, is limping now. Long years ahead of him, and he loves the game. Does he have something else to keep him alive?

---

1   "Bilal" is the name given him when he became a Muslim at the prison. He is out, and his first Sunday out he visited the church I pastor in Mill Valley and spoke from the pulpit for about a half hour.

38

Guards at the Gates

"Bulls," "turn keys," "screws"—these terms I have never heard at San Quentin. Not that they are not used; it is just that I have never heard them. "Cops," "C Os," (short for Correctional Officers), "officers," and "guards" are the terms normally used—that is, unless someone is a sergeant, lieutenant, captain, associate warden, deputy warden, and of course, warden.

Convicts call the guards by their last names. My usual term is officer when I am addressing one of them; sometimes I say sir or ma'am, probably due to my time in the military. When I am talking to an inmate about a C O, I will say guard or cop.

There are two gates that must be entered to get to the lower yard and the Field of Dreams. The East Gate is across from the San Quentin Village post office, connected to two raunchy, I mean really raunchy bath rooms. Sandwiched in between the toilets and the gate is a store where prisoner handicrafts are sold. Sadly, it is rarely open, but when it is, the store clerk is a convict dressed in a yellow jumpsuit. Over the years I have bought some high-quality items there, quite inexpensive. My favorite piece is the construction, in miniature, of a cell on condemned row.[1]

There is also a West Gate that is used for the big rigs that keep the prison supplied.

East Gate: There is a smallish booth there, always occupied by a guard. This guard has a handgun hanging from a belt; the only other guns you will see at the prison are rifles carried by guards in the wall posts or towers sprinkled appropriately around the place. He, and occasionally she, control all the traffic coming in via vehicles driven by officers and other staff coming into the prison. A car approaches, the guard opens a large iron gate, and the officer will wave it in when the credentials are identified.

---

1   One time, in front of a few of the guys on the team I referred to "death row." Quickly I was reminded that the term is "condemned row."

Years ago, there was what was called the Scope Gate, directly across the main road from the warden's office, which is right in front of the count gate. There was a very sensitive machine there, like those at airports now, and it was necessary to take off your shoes, too. It is not operating now; there is a sign on the door that says, "Lactation station." There is a padlock on the door, which has been there for years. Not much lactating going on.

Count Gate: Once inside the count gate and through the sally port you are now inside the prison. On your right as you enter is the Captain's Porch, which you want to stay away from and only go there if absolutely necessary. Continuing right is the Catholic Chapel, which is next to the Protestant Garden Chapel. Probably not original, but now attached to the Protestant Chapel are several different offices. One is where the American Indian chapel clerk has an office, and then in a building joined at a right angle to the chapel is another one used by the Jews and the Muslims. Who knows these things?

On the left side, as one enters the prison from the count gate, is a memorial to fallen officers, killed in the line of duty. Directly behind that is the Adjustment Center, a prison within a prison. Convicts having received a capital sentence go there when they first arrive, so they can learn how to live in a place where the only way they will leave is in a casket. The adjustment may take two or more years. It is also a home for very violent criminals, those who are obviously dangerous. This brief description is only a part of it. Over the years I have both seen and heard a lot of things that go on around the Adjustment Center, but it would not be wise for me to write about any of that.

There are three watches: first watch is 10 p.m. to 6 a.m.; second watch, 6 a.m. to 2 p.m.; and third watch, 2 p.m. to 10 p.m. The third watch guards, during the weekdays, are the interesting ones.

I have been told that the prison picks the biggest jerks among the hundreds of guards to work at the gates. This is so in some cases—I will risk saying that much. At the East Gate, third watch on weekdays, is a guard I cannot figure out. At times he is harsh and punishing, yet at other times he is very cooperative. At the Count Gate, for the last year or so, third watch, week days, is a guard who could only be described as unhappy, disgruntled, angry, and unpleasant. But there is one guard, the worst anyone has ever seen, and I will not mention the shift or days he works the Count Gate. He is truly unbelievable and someone I would fire right now if I could. He is known throughout the prison, by guards and convicts alike, as "jerk cop number one." The convicts would never have occasion to be in personal contact with him. Let me give you an example.

Two weeks ago, I brought a team in, about fifteen guys, all with equipment bags, and found this particular officer at the count gate. I stepped up first, set my equipment bag down, presented by "beige card" or volunteer identifying card down for him to see, and then proceeded to sign the visitor control sheet. He handed me a slip of paper with the word, "Inventory" written on it. I was to take every item out of my bag, inventory the contents, repack it and wait. I did. He took the now signed sheet and went through my bag, every item, to see that my inventory account was correct. He did this with every single player. Nearly one hour later we are almost to the lower yard. After the game, exiting, the bags had to be emptied again and each item matched against the list.

For each game I bring in the baseballs to be used for the game. These are stashed in the front compartment of the bag. Coming in there were twelve game balls; coming out there were five. What happened to the seven missing balls? It sounded like it was going to be a big deal.

"They are in PIA," I answered. PIA, Prison Industry Authority, where all kinds of stuff is made by the inmates for the prisons around the state, and between PIA and the ball field is a huge yellow brick wall and balls hit over it are rarely seen again, since one of the free men who works there has a kid in little league, and being the good dad that he is he makes donations.

The guard thought about it while I stood there trying not to show any attitude. Without a word he zipped up the ball compartment and motioned me out the door.

Outside team coming in from the East Gate to Count Gate

39
The Last Double Header

Saturday, September 28: the Giants were scheduled to play the Stanislaus Storm in the morning and the All Blacks in the evening. The Storm had a three-hour drive to the prison; their manager was worried about not having enough players, so we processed four more of his players during the week. To get the new names checked through the national database was far from easy, forcing me to ask for a special favor. Friday morning the manager emailed a cancellation—only five players could make the trip.

If not for email, there would have been no game at all, but between the Willing and a blanket email to all the coaches I had in my baseball folder, we got seven players, enough to make it happen. From the Giants, I sent over Marcus Crumb to catch and Charles Lyons to play the outfield; these guys are usually on the bench, so it was a rare good opportunity for them to play a whole game.

The first game

A young man named Sam, who hadn't pitched in eight months, cruised through seven innings and held us to one run while they scored seven. The Giants couldn't hit, couldn't field, and Johnny, our very excellent catcher, threw two pick off attempts into right field and one into left. That accounted for five runs total.

Henry, who is headed home to Oakland in a few months, wanted to start one more ball game. He got the loss but didn't deserve it. For some reason Johnny was firing from his knees and missing badly. I could hardly wait for the game to be over.

This now was the second game in a row we had lost. Twice before the loss total had gone to four in a row. Our overall record was very good—twenty wins versus eleven losses and one tie—but things get funny quick.

We had few base runners, so I could not work my small ball game—bunts, steals, hit and run, and my favorites, squeezes and pickles.

The Phenom, no longer, hadn't gotten a hit in a long while. If it had not been for his defense, he would have been a fixture on the bench. I thought of using a designated hitter for him but decided he might not be able to handle the disappointment.

I had heard he had blamed me for his poor hitting. After his fourth homer in three games, I mentioned to him that he had a shot at breaking the old thirteen home run San Quentin record. In retrospect he might have been right, too; it got into his head; he began trying too hard, resorted to a sweeping, looping softball swing he was used to, as almost all convicts do who play a lot of softball, and it was merely an accident when he even made contact with a pitched ball. Lamarr—that is the real name of the Phenom—was showing up late for games and not getting in his warmups. He was on a slide down hill, and everyone knew it.

Sam, the pitcher who started for the patched up outside team, ran out of gas after seven, Eric came in, and we got to him for four runs. Last of the ninth we got the tying run to the plate, then we hit a wall and the game ended. Some of the guys did not take it well and started blaming the obvious guys, even Johnny, the team leader.

Marcus, who caught for the visiting team, played one heck of a ball game behind the plate and hit even better. Charles didn't hit a thing but caught everything hit his direction. At least I was not embarrassed by their play.

We did do a half-hearted high-five lineup with the other team then gathered at the mound. Briefly I thanked the visitors for responding to the SOS and talked about a couple of game highlights. Dave, our team chaplain, had a visitor, so I figured Frankie would lead the prayer, but I was wrong. Duck stepped to the top of the mound, took off his cap, placed it over his heart, and invited any who would to bow their heads for a prayer. I was shocked as I heard a nicely worded and thoughtful prayer come out of this three-striker. You just never know about some of the guys.

The second game

By the time I got to the count gate it was 1 p.m., home by 1:15 and back at 4:20. At age sixty-eight, it is a bit of a stretch. Will Harris and the All Blacks were in the lower parking lot; there were only seven of them, just like in the morning. Oh well, at least we would have a game.

Almost a carbon copy of Sam at the morning game, Will's pitcher, a tall young skinny kid named Trevor, threw real hard and could hit his spots.

Mario started for my Giants and was shaky at first. At the end of two we were behind by two. He settled down and breezed through the next five innings, but by the end of the seventh, which would be the last of it due to the 8 p.m. count, we were not yet on the board. Three losses in a row loomed large.

The frustration had showed up in the third inning. Chris Marshall, who could be described as a smoldering volcano, was yelling at guys, and they were yelling back. Even Bilal, the Rock, who is one of the most dependable players, was barking and blaming. During the bottom of the third I had to leave the third base coaching box twice to stop the angry trash talk coming from the dugout. Duck, who had earlier prayed a great prayer, got thrown out of the game for arguing a called third strike. (Funny, Duck is a three-striker with a fifty-year sentence. Doubt there is any connection.) More than once, I have been surprised that the cons allow me to order them around when they could easily silence me. During that second game I was reminded that I do what I do with the convicts' permission.

James Bautista cutting off a throw from Duck Harris

Johnny of the three errant throws in the first game was also catching the second game. No question he was tired. He was not hitting, and as team captain was supposed to be keeping the guys in line, but they were ignoring him. During the bottom of the fifth, I saw another eruption coming, and by the time I got into the dugout to stop the yelling, Johnny had left the dugout, sitting alongside the fence along left field, and was busy taking off his cleats.

I walked back out onto the field, walked to where he was seated but with the fence between us and I bent over and said, "Johnny, this game may depend on your throwing a runner out at second." That was it; I went to the box to coach and didn't look back. I did not know for sure what would happen, until I saw Johnny standing in the on deck circle a little later on. Whew!

Bottom of the seventh, which would be our last at bat, did not start out well—one man out and no one on. Our leadoff batter, James Bautista, our fastest man and best base runner, looped a single to left. He promptly stole second with me working small ball. It was one of those times I was either going to look like a genius or a jerk, and it wasn't up to me which. Any call made in baseball is based on some logic and chance—you know, a rock in the way, a gust of wind, and so on—and on execution, meaning the ability of a player to make a play. Three components—and all three need to go right and will make the difference between being a hero or an asshole. And the latter I did not want to be, desperately did not want to be.

Left: Terry Burton was for years a "Peer Counselor," one of a handful on inmates who helped new inmates make adjustment to prison life. Out now, he was involved with the baseball team longer than another player and coach. Looking forward to meeting up with him.

James on second, but we needed three runs, two to tie, which I would take. Second man up was Marcus, our reserve catcher I had as an EH, extra hitter. He placed a bunt between the pitcher and the first baseman and beat the throw to first. Now James on third, Marcus on first. Second pitch to Johnny, hitting third and thankfully still in the game, got one up into the outfield. James tagged and we were one run behind. Two out, man on first. Redd, hitting fourth, took a wild pitch and Marcus was on second. Then, without being given the steal sign, he stole third on the next pitch. The opposition walked Redd intentionally, of course, and I had Chris Marshall run for him. Yes, having Chris run for Redd was not quite Kosher, but the whole game had been like that, so I didn't feel like a cheater. Now I gave Chris the pickle sign indicator—hand to the bill of the cap, then six taps on the arm—he is to get caught in a run down between first and second and not get tagged out until the runner from third scores. In that case, we have a tie.

Right: The big ole guy (Dave Baker) coming in hard to third base. I am coaching at third.

Perfectly done, Chris takes off while the pitcher is looking in for a sign, but no one notices. Terry Burton, one smart baseball guy, yells out of our dugout to the pitcher about the guy off the base. The pitcher whirls around, sees Chris and runs at him and flips the ball to the second baseman. Marcus is off, I mean going, and barely slides under the catcher's tag. Tie game. Chris alertly comes all the way around to third. Now there is a chance to win.

At this point the lineup has been so stirred around that the fifth hitter, normally a good bat, is on the bench and a weak hitter is up. The best chance is for another passed ball or wild pitch. Chris and I confer, and he knows it all might be up to him. Fortunately, the pitcher is taking a full windup and not holding him on. Chris has a short fuse but does know the game. He takes a moderate lead, then with the pitch takes a hard secondary lead. Our break comes on the fifth pitch, two balls and two strikes, a curve ball that skips by the catcher. Chris breaks, the catcher wheels to retrieve the ball, the pitcher coming hard to take a throw, and Chris is almost there. The ball and the runner get there seemingly at the same time. Nick the umpire waves safe. Who knows, but right or wrong, there it is. A win.

Lineup for high fives, not time for a speech or a prayer, only time to collect the uniforms and the gear to be put back in the green metal locker box and the players back in their cells. What a day, sixteen innings of baseball; lose one win one.

40
Oakland

Private and personal conversations are not frequent during a baseball season, and when one happens it is usually during the late innings of a boring and seemingly endless game. During the month of August, we had two such games, and I came to know Henry and Marcus better than I ever had before.

Henry (see two photos of him in chapter 32) has played on three of my teams. A big, friendly, quiet-spoken man, handsome, shy, black, and from Oakland. My guess is he is about thirty years old. He does not look like a gang banger, hoodlum type, not even close. I have thought that something rather unusual had brought him to prison. He will be paroled in December, one of our few non-lifers or three-strikers.

Marcus (see a photo of him in chapter 28)—first year with the baseball program at SQ and no doubt not the last, but he may have to play for the No Name team. He is a gang banger and a member of a truly sinister gang. He is black, not shy, not handsome necessarily, thin and wiry, about twenty-six, and he is also from Oakland. Marcus is a three striker with a very long sentence.

What I am hoping to do here is present a composite summary of what I heard these two men say to me over the course of several innings of baseball. Both men, though their circumstances were different from each other, related a similar picture of how they saw themselves in terms of their past, present, and possible future. Let it be understood that I have no political axe to grind, and I am not sophisticated sociologically. Perhaps there is some value in what comes next, but I am not sure what it could be.

Oakland is an island in the midst of a gigantic sea—a world apart, a dangerous place to grow up a city where a black underclass has been invaded by immigrants from south of the border. Where once the black gangs received shipments of all manner of drugs originating in Mexico or beyond and made their money distributing the goods to their customers, the Norteños, Sureños, and Border Brothers, all three large Mexican gangs, well armed, organized, and trained, saw no reason to act merely as middlemen—they wanted all the profits. War then went on between the Mexicans and the Blacks and between the various gangs within each racial grouping. High stakes—millions of dollars flowed up and down the streets.

If a con returned to Oakland, and there was no other alternative while on parole (or probably ever), there was no way to develop a separate existence apart from the gangs. It would not happen, at least for Henry and Marcus.

Graffiti in Oakland (by L. M. Clancy)

What about moving away? Slim chance, as there would be relatives to care for and maybe even a wife or girl friend, or a boy friend. Move away? Where and how? Not an option, as neither the resources nor opportunities would likely ever be there. An ex-con does not simply hit the road and live off the land doing small jobs and camping out in the parks.

Get a job? A convict in the midst of a city that is mostly shut down to the day laborer, for a guy with a felony conviction and time in a state prison, for a black man with no skills, there would be no job. San Francisco across the bridge—no reliable transportation and who would hire a guy who looked like and acted like and talked like he had just gotten out of the joint?

Besides, what to do with the gang tattoos?

What about clothes? The $200 given to each convict released from prison would not last long. Clothes are a big deal, and due to the gangs, the colors red, blue, and black are out. How angry a young person gets seeing all around him people dressed in flashy clothes and driving nice cars, and they have nothing or next to it. The anger of going without is not easily overcome and can become a force powerful enough to push one to do things one would not ordinarily do.

Left: Kent and Chris Rich, out now several years and doing very well, owns a home.

A young man gets restless with no sports programs going, not to mention a job, though plenty of groups get non-profit status, get on television about some program to help the poor, then the money from the grants and loans is mostly gone by the time the activists pay themselves salaries and benefits. These do-gooders come and go on a regular basis.

Life in Oakland is boring; sounds like the complaint of a teenager, but there is nothing much to do. Street life is at least somewhat exciting—hanging out, getting drunk or high or both, making some money the easy way, the possibility of some sex one way or the other, and the subtle chill of danger just being on the street. Even contact with cops and courts are not all that bad—at least it breaks up the monotony. In prison there is baseball and other sports, and baseball lasts half a year.

Get married and settle down with a wife and kids? Well, not really. There is no job and no money. The black women are having kids all right, but kids and fathers are not easy to match up, and that black woman can survive with kids as long as she remains single. Our system takes its toll.

Why is AIDS such a big deal in black neighborhoods? Why do local jails have condom dispensaries available—a young man is going to have sex with somebody, and rape often lands you back in jail.

After a while, it is better to hustle on the street and take your chances, even if you die young. What difference does it make anyway? Prison time would even be a break, where one could get some rest, some medical attention, and learn better ways to make a living—in Oakland.

Right:

John Neblett, long time equipment manager, played some also, wanted to be a pitcher. Out now for some years, developed into a very good Shakespearean actor. Several years ago, he organized a get together for former SQ players and coaches. We communicate from time to time.

Below:

Coach discussing with the home plate umpire, SQ "fans" in the background.

41
Where's Dishon?

Cons lie. Let me rephrase: Most cons lie.

They know they do, and they cultivate the art. If you are up to no good, it will not work to tell the truth. This is not a treatise on developmental psychology, but if I am any example, the lying starts early.

At age eight I stole a deck of cards from the Fred Myers store on Union St. (now Martin Luther King Jr. Blvd.) and NE Portland Blvd. in Portland, Oregon. Mom wanted to know where I got it. Change would disappear from my dad's copper bowl he made when he worked in the shipyards in Portland during WWII. So, I learned how to lie. "It wasn't me" came in handy. And I wasn't even a sociopath.

"I can throw the ball 100 miles an hour."

"Really?" "Yep, right now, too."

"Let me get us a ball and a couple of gloves and let's see it."

Was I hearing a lie or evidence of a separate reality? Very hard to know.

"I played major league baseball." "Wow, what organization?" "Oh, you know, big league stuff."

Sincere, looking me right in the eye, hoping for whatever. Lie upon lie and often over the course of a whole season. It is no use challenging the information, as even more lies will be piled on top.

Dishon was an expert. After I figured it out, I realized that the whole time we had been engaged in meaningful conversation I was being fed an increasingly complicated web of falsehoods, all designed to make the young man look good. But he could not keep up the façade.

I was disappointed. I had been duped again, thinking this guy could do something on the outside and he would be released in a year or two. We talked about him getting hooked up with one of the teams that come into the prison, and maybe one day he could come in playing against our Giants. He was all smiles.

Let me tell you the extent to which I was conned. I bought, with my own money, a nice set of baseball cleats for him as well as let him use my very best glove. Once he quit the team, I heard he had sold the gear to the highest bidder off the tier in North Block. When I reported that to the team (there are few secrets on the baseball field) the items showed up a week later, actually brought back by Dishon who apologized for his behavior. Right, there is mystery here.

What do I think about Dishon now, who by the way gave me permission to tell this story, and what have I learned from the experience?

Cons lie. It is habitual—some know it and some don't. "Who are you?" "Well, I am a scumbag loser, who has spent his life robbing, raping, and pillaging anyone I could." Or, and maybe closer to reality, "I was raised by my aunt, never knew my father, was abused when I was five, then more when I was thirteen, went to a lockup when I was fifteen, graduated when I turned twenty-one, then made it here on a murder beef. Gonna be here awhile." Maybe a lie would have worked better.

It might be necessary to lie, mostly to yourself, if for no other reason than to have a mechanism in place to keep from being a suicide or losing your mind.

Prison is worse than most think. Even youth get over bragging about their prison time, having supposed that others think it is cool to have served time in San Quentin. I wish it carried a bigger stigma than it does in some communities.

My conclusion is that Dishon lied to keep from going crazy. A few of the men over the years have reported that they can feel it happening to them, sense they are sliding into a world of lies they have invented for themselves, because the pain of what has happened is too much to contemplate. Reinventing yourself works for a while as a defense mechanism.

Most guys make peace with their minds and emotions and thereby avoid going on psych meds, which carries with it additional stigma. This season two players I know of have been on the meds,[1] and it's apparent from time to time. I would never bring it up to them, however.

Dishon is still at the prison. Wonder what next season will bring.[2]

---

1   I observed this because, standing at the MAC Shack by North Block when the North Block residents are allowed to go to chow, those who are on meds, along with the diabetics, come out first. Frankly, I wish I had not been there to see it, for those guys and for me. However, I do applaud them for reaching out for help.

2   2020: Dishon is now home, and I am not sure when that happened.

Left:

Rico Liboy, a fine young man is how I saw him. Loved being on the team. A real asset.

Above and Left: Curtis Roberts

Curtis, starting second baseman and leadoff hitter for several years. After 29 years, he is out, lives nearby, and we talk often. Last year I performed his wedding to Lora. He works with high school and college kids about how to stay outside of prison, trouble, and suicide.

42
21 Wins, 12 Losses, 1 Tie

The season is over, and I am not unhappy about it. We did have a winning season, though I must admit we played some rather poor teams. Oh well, we played baseball, and that is the whole deal.

Seven months, at least two days a week, but it is doing the gate clearances that drags me down. Almost every day comes an email or a phone call—a question about whether a player got cleared, and if not, why not. While not exactly digging ditches, dealing with the outside teams is more like a constant and annoying drip of a leaky faucet. I am so glad the teams come in, since that makes all the difference, but it is not simply done.

There was one last game—the Giants versus the No Name team. The other players did not want to be called anything in particular, so everyone called them the No Name team, until they finally adopted it.

This game was a concession on my part. So far here, I have not let on what was really taking place all season, but now I am letting it all out—maybe therapy for me.

After the tryouts were concluded the first week of March, there were a whole group of guys who did not make the team. Then there were others who felt they could not come out because they were in programs they needed, because they wanted to get out of prison, and programs look good to the parole board. But then there were guys who simply refused to play for me—or to put it more accurately, they did not like me.

The pressure started due to one inmate who is now out of prison after twenty-nine years down, and to whom I had made concessions.

It is not exactly like I have a lot of power at SQ, but I have acquired a certain amount of leeway and can get some things done. The safety valve, I figured, would be an intramural baseball program. There were enough players left over, and so on, to make it work. I asked one of our coaches to take it over, since there needed to be a sponsor. It looked like a good fit, and all seemed fine. But then more pressure started coming my way.

The intramural guys wanted to play the Giants. Okay, easy, a practice game for the team now and then. That worked for two weeks, then another demand surfaced—they wanted to play outside teams just like the Giants.

Again, I made a concession—okay, maybe a few games. Not good enough, though. Now the rumor floated around that next year, 2011, the No Name team would be a team like the Giants and have their own schedule and everything.

I called the guy who had volunteered to run the program. After an extremely frustrating conversation I concluded that he had caved in to the cons. This is not the first time I have seen this happen. Convicts have a lot of "con" in them, and more than one volunteer has gotten conned. How it works is the volunteer wants to be liked and appreciated by the inmates and then begins to take the convicts' side. I have seen some volunteers taken away in handcuffs as a result, having been caught bringing in all kinds of stuff including cell phones and drugs.

Meetings and more meetings were held with the state employees who oversee the recreation program—not much fun, a waste of time, and I threatened—yes, I threatened to take it to the warden. I had all kinds of reasons, some of which were probably good ones, to bring up to the higher authorities along custody lines, meaning that all the additional outside teams coming in would pose certain problems.

Back to the last game—it did not count in terms of the record, but on September 1, the Giants played the No Name team one last time. So as not to later be accused of a lack of fairness, there was a coin toss to see who got to be home team. The Giants won so we had our usual dugout.

Nick, the regular umpire, the one convict who bucked the boycott that occurred when I refused to let one certain con ump, had been released from the prison (much to my surprise), and no one could be found to call balls and strikes. Kevin was going to manage the game, and since there was not much for me to do, I agreed to ump from behind the pitcher's mound. (I had no cup, so I was not going to put on the gear and get behind the catcher, and besides, I would never trust the No Name team catcher to do his job—payback you know.)

Amazingly, it was a whole lot of fun. Both teams played well, with the Giants winning the game after six good innings, 4 to 2. A few calls could have gone either way, but for the most part it was a clean game. I did not start feeling all warm and fuzzy about the guys we beat, but I began to think differently about the baseball program.

Left:

In the dugout: Charles Lyons, Dave Baker, Chris Rich, and Keving Loughlin

Below:

End of game high-fives

Above: Bottom of the 6th inning: Terry Burton slides unsuccessfully into second base. Below: Kevin Driscoll pitching the top of the 7th inning with the Giants behind by five runs.

Above: More activity from opening day (fans, photographers, and tennis players in the background)

Below: High Fives Closeup

43
A Mother and Daughter

Not that I intend to break the rules, but it happens. There have been occasions when I brought in a baseball glove or a pair of cleats without filling out a donation form. The process can take months; paperwork has been known to go missing. The reality is that when a player has no glove or cleats, and no chance of acquiring any through the normal channels—a rule might be broken.

Selfishly, I don't let any of the other coaches do this. It would be one thing for me to be reprimanded, maybe lose my volunteer card. But it would be worse if I should make a need known, expecting someone to fulfill it, and have the whole thing go awry.

Another situation, and more dangerous, is contact with the family of a convict. Players have asked me to speak with a family member. My answer has been no. I explain why, but the convict knows the situation already. It is not that the prison system is against such a thing, but it can put me in a difficult place. What if I am asked to bring in some sort of contraband or pass a message along? Worse, be threatened into facilitating for or arranging for an exchange to be made in the visitor's room during a normal visit. Over the years, I have resisted speaking or meeting with family members, but I did do it once, just at the end of the season.

A player that had been on several Giants teams was suicidal, and everyone knew, since he spoke of it openly. A three-striker, he would die in prison, given his age and the number of years he had to do. Then, after ten or so years down, a cancerous tumor showed up in his neck. Since my brother is a survivor of head and neck cancer, I knew something about its process and progressive invasion.

A couple of times a year the man's mother and young daughter came to visit him from another state. They did not have much money, and the trip, transportation, lodging, and food for two people was not easily managed. He had so far not been able to tell his mother about the cancer and the likelihood, given the state of the medical care he was receiving, or not receiving, that he would not live too much longer. He wanted me to break the news.

At first, I said no. A month went by, and he approached me again during a team practice. This time I said that I wished I could. That night I was troubled and thought about the mother and the daughter. I knew something of the pain and suffering a mother goes through with a precious child locked up and beyond her capacity to be a mother to him again. And the daughter—growing up with her father in prison, never able to have him in her life, with her mother dead, in this case from a drug overdose. I changed my mind.

Next time out to the prison would be a game, and I would find a time to talk to the player and let him know I was ready to do what he asked.

Let me call him Ed. Ed was white, a northern California meth head, arrested over and over for sales and running a meth lab. His front teeth were mostly gone though he was only thirty-five years old. Skinny, as most speed freaks are, he hid a soft side inside a hard shell. It took me years to even like him. He was not talkative, and few of the other players liked him, but he was left-handed, threw side arm, and threw strikes. He got into almost every other game for an inning, maybe two.

Ed did not show up for the game, or the next or the next. No one seemed to know what happened to him. Without warning he walked up behind me while I was sitting in the dugout. He looked sick and I knew instantly his season was over, and I thought maybe his life would soon be over, too. He asked me quietly if I would please reconsider talking to his mother, and I said that I had already decided to do it.

He handed me a slip of paper with a phone number on it, smiled a thin smile and walked away. I have not seen him since.

When I made the call, a woman who sounded ancient answered, and after some confusion and time, she finally grasped who I was. Saying as little as possible, I was careful that she write down my phone number and invited her to call me when she next visited her son. She said she would.

With just a week left in the season she called. Near the prison is an extensive series of high-end shops at an open mall, and the Marin Brewing Company is there where often I meet with visiting ball clubs for a burger and a pint of good beer after a game. She did not know how to Google the address and get a map, so I gave her detailed instructions on how to get there.

Two weeks after the season was over, making it the second Saturday in September, the three of us were sitting at an outside table at the restaurant. The mother looked as tired as she had sounded on the phone, and the little girl, Ed's daughter, about ten years old, was sad-eyed and very quiet.

It was one thing to give bad news to a mother about her son, but telling a young girl about the soon coming death of her father was another. In the rush of things in my crazy life, I had not processed how it might be to have the girl there. I did not know how to approach the subject, so I kept quiet about what I was there for. We just talked about small stuff.

Watching and Waiting – What Will Happen Next?

I was not going to be able to bring it up in front of the little girl. The only thing I could think of was, when I walked the two out to their rented car, I would get the girl seated in the car then speak to the mother out of earshot. Not the best of course, but the better possibility. The plan worked, in that the girl did not hear me tell the mother about her father. The mother said she suspected this would be what she would hear and thanked me for not talking about it openly. She would see to that at the proper time.

It was far more business-like than I thought it would be. The poor woman shed no tears—probably those had already been shed, but the tired look seemed to deepen. How I wanted to make everything okay or at least be of more help than what I had been. Driving home I thought about the sadness that permeates our living and the losses that we inevitably experience. How we handle these realities and keep from giving into cynicism and sadness I do not know. Again, I realized some of the hidden costs of being involved with a prison.

Below: Permanently stenciled on the lower yard pavement, beyond which the convicts are not allowed to go.

44

Baseball and the Search for Meaning

Wasted years?
   The time slips away. Twelve years down. Twenty years down. Thirty years have passed, and the hair has gone grey, the teeth are ugly and some are missing, parents are gone now, friends have stopped writing and visiting, never had a wife or family. Yet, the search for meaning, to have a mission, must continue.

I return to the "mission" theme, since the search for meaning often dominates the thought life of prisoners. To have nowhere to go, little to do, and no pleasant daydreams popping into one's mind anymore, is one dreadful battle to fight day after day.

There are some distractions. Chow—but many hate it and prefer to fix their own meals, however meager, in their cells. Recipes are exchanged; unusual food stuffs are sold and swapped. One Asian inmate caught, killed, and smuggled a full-grown Canadian goose[1] into his cell and boiled it in oil in a contraption cleverly built. He got caught, and I guess never got to eat the bird, which was too bad. There is a hobby shop, all sorts of classes to take, the chapels to attend and be involved with, veterans organizations, 12-Step programs, and a lot more—at San Quentin anyway, since it is located in a large metropolitan area—and there is recreation.

The baseball program is only one of many opportunities to find meaning. A player must learn to cooperate with others, work at getting in athletic shape, cope with losing—which there is more of than in most sports—and compete against peers. This is certainly a short list; another worth mentioning is developing an interest in the sport itself by following one of the local major league teams, the Giants and the A's. The convicts have access to the

---

[1] Flocks of geese can be found on the Field of Dreams nearly all year long. It is against policy to disturb, feed, or harm one of them. These animals poop everywhere and make playing the outfield an adventure. The flag football team especially detests the geese.

Marin Independent Journal and the *San Francisco Chronicle*. Many of the guys follow the teams in detail, and the twists and turns of are of intense interest to them. As it is said, "This is a good thing."

More than the pro teams, the players dwell on the home team, their San Quentin Giants. Often, I lose sight of this and err in taking the game and the team too lightly—or even worse, I can begin, especially toward the end of the season, to see it as something akin to work, a job I have to do.

The season is done now and the photos handed out. Oh, how the guys love the photos! Right now, as I finish up the story of the 2010 San Quentin Giants Baseball Season, I remember the looks in the eyes of the players as I handed each man a legal sized brown envelope with the team picture, three each, and photos of them in action on the ball field. Some got more than others, not intentionally, and each picture will be to them more than I will ever see or know. The photos will be proof of something they did, in their youth, sort of, a memento to tack up on the cell wall, send to a parent or a son or daughter, a reminder maybe that their life has some meaning to it.

Right:

Bill Mauck, my old-time high school buddy. We played baseball together at Verdugo Hill High School in Los Angeles during the 1950s. Bill took most of the action shots in this book.

Above: Keeping Score — Below: End of Game Prayer

Looking east toward San Quentin State Prison, as seen across the tidal lagoon next to Highway 101 in Corte Madera, California, Marin County.

Below: Fans lined up to watch baseball with the new hospital, built in 2009, in the background.

SAN QUENTIN GIANTS BASEBALL TEAM 2010

(from left to right, back row) Elliot Smith, coach; Stan Damas, coach; Kevin Loughlin, coach; Kevin Driscoll, Drew Scholler, John Neblett, James Bautista, Dave Baker, Redd Casey, Chris Marshall, Chris Rich, Matt White, Kevin Henry; Lamarr King, Bilal Chatman, Mario Ellis, Frankie Smith, Mike Deeble, coach; Kent Philpott, coach

(front row) Terry Burton, Johnny Taylor, Stafont Smith, Charles Lyons, Rico Liboy, Mike Tyler, Orlando Harris, Curtis Roberts, Dominique Oden, Marcus Crumb

Season Record: 21 wins 12 losses 1 tie

Pitchers Records:		Home Runs:	
Dave Baker	0 and 3	Redd Casey	4
Terry Burton	1 and 0	Kevin Driscoll	3
Kevin Driscoll	7 and 2	Mario Ellis	2
Mario Ellis	6 and 3	Kevin Henry	2
Kevin Henry	3 and 1	Lamarr King	4
Rico Liboy	1 and 0		
Chris Rich	2 and 1		
Matt White	1 and 2		

167

168

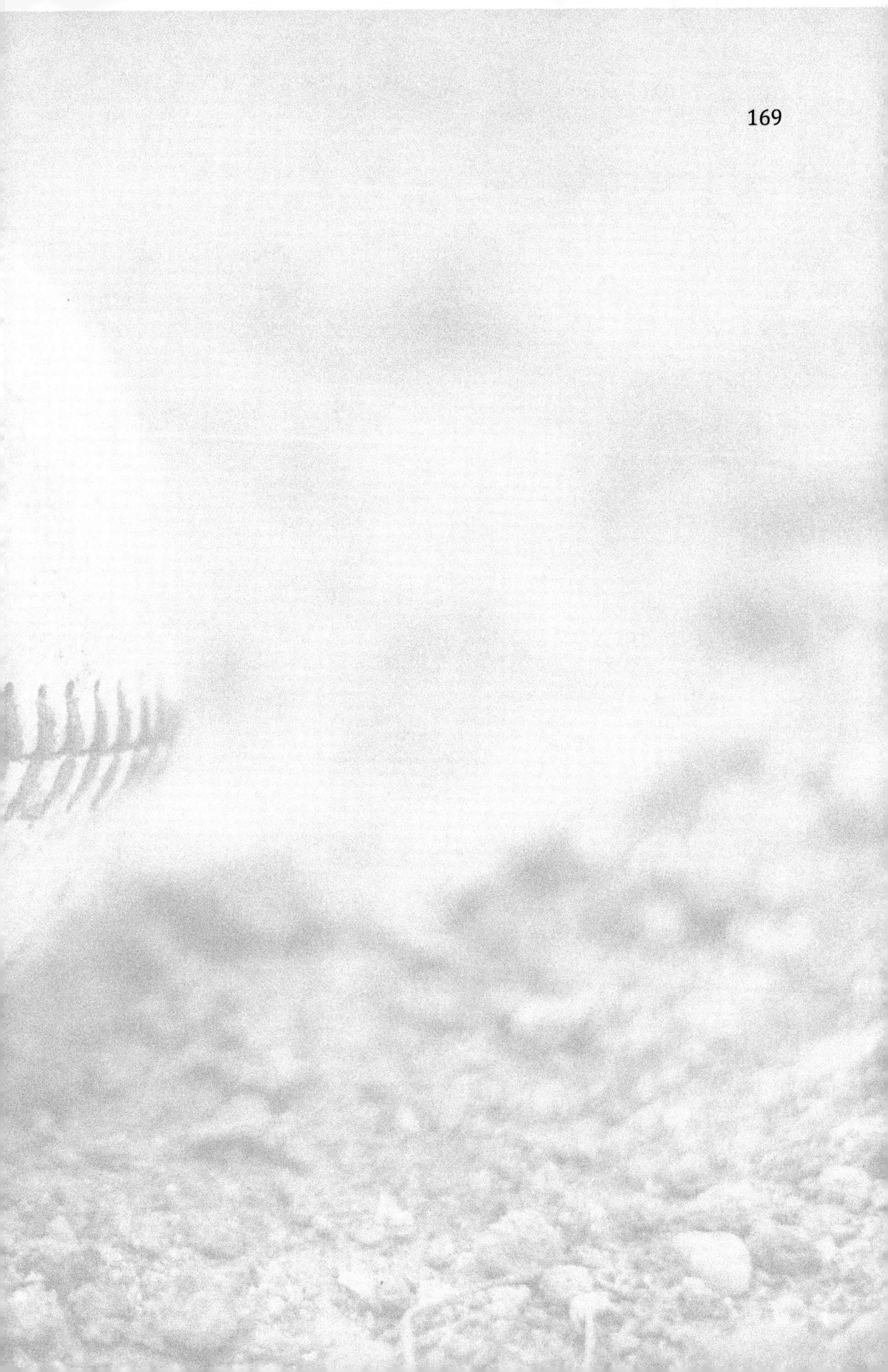

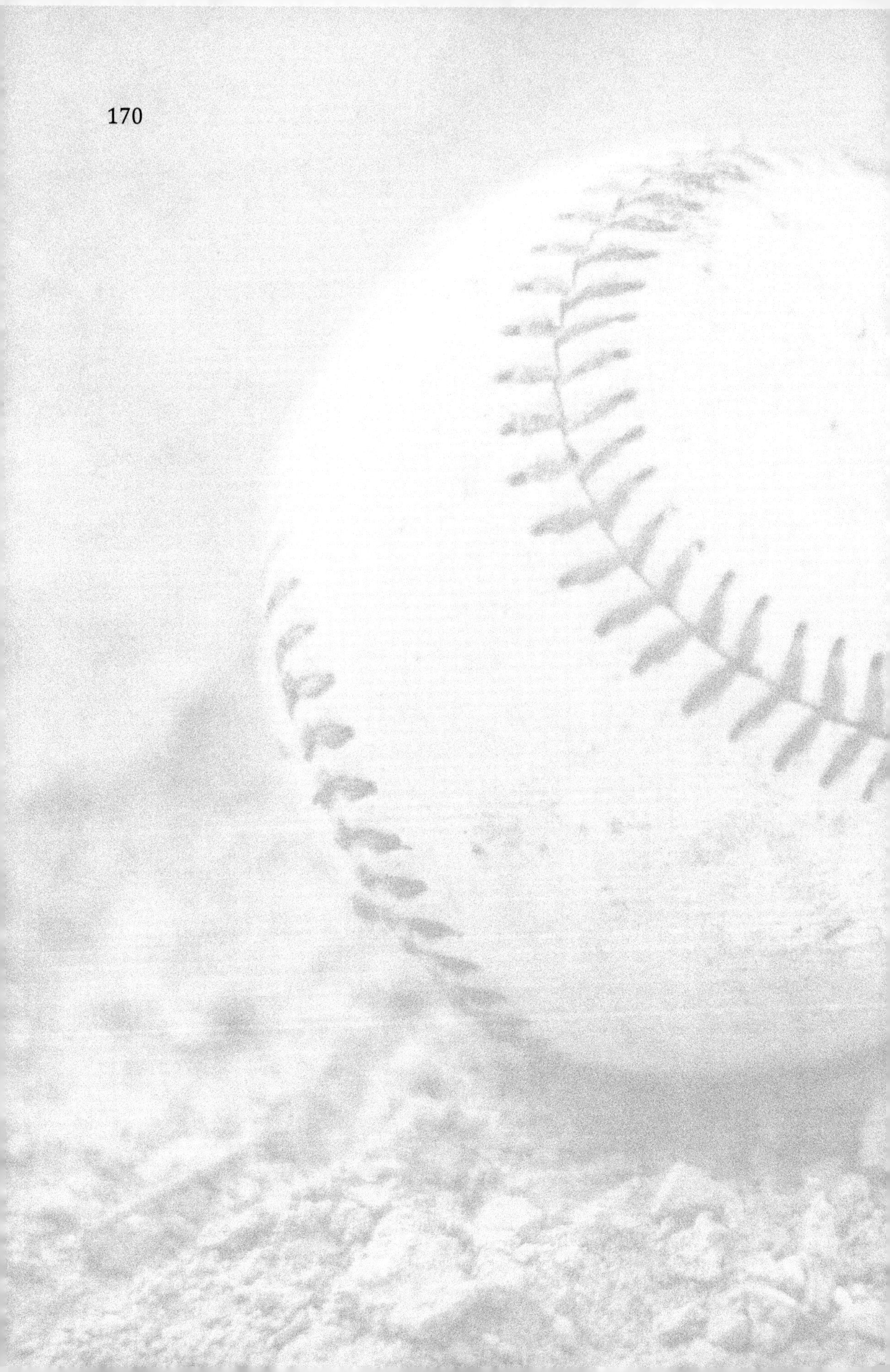